Health Care

Other Books in the Current Controversies Series

Health Care

Noël Merino, Book Editor

GREENHAVEN PRESS
A part of Gale, Cengage Learning

Detroit • New York • San Francisco • New Haven, Conn • Waterville, Maine • London

GALE
CENGAGE Learning™

Christine Nasso, *Publisher*
Elizabeth Des Chenes, *Managing Editor*

© 2011 Greenhaven Press, a part of Gale, Cengage Learning

Gale and Greenhaven Press are registered trademarks used herein under license.

For more information, contact:
Greenhaven Press
27500 Drake Rd.
Farmington Hills, MI 48331-3535
Or you can visit our Internet site at gale.cengage.com

For product information and technology assistance, contact us at

Gale Customer Support, 1-800-877-4253
For permission to use material from this text or product, submit all requests online at www.cengage.com/permissions

Further permissions questions can be emailed to permissionrequest@cengage.com

Articles in Greenhaven Press anthologies are often edited for length to meet page requirements. In addition, original titles of these works are changed to clearly present the main thesis and to explicitly indicate the author's opinion. Every effort is made to ensure that Greenhaven Press accurately reflects the original intent of the authors. Every effort has been made to trace the owners of copyrighted material.

Cover image copyright Julián Rovagnati, 2010. Used under license from Shutterstock.com.

LIBRARY OF CONGRESS CATALOGING-IN-PUBLICATION DATA

Health care / Noël Merino, book editor.
    p. cm. -- (Current controversies)
    Includes bibliographical references and index.
    ISBN 978-0-7377-5099-7 (hardcover) -- ISBN 978-0-7377-5100-0 (pbk.)
    1. Medical care--United States. 2. Health care reform--United States. I. Merino, Noël.
    RA395.A3H3857 2010
    362.1--dc22
                                                    2010027455

Printed in the United States of America
1 2 3 4 5 6 7 14 13 12 11 10

Contents

Chapter 3: Would a Public Health Insurance Option Be Beneficial?

Reforming the health care system through a single-payer plan would perpetuate the outdated components of the current system and worsen health care.

Foreword

By definition, controversies are "discussions of questions in which opposing opinions clash" (Webster's Twentieth Century Dictionary Unabridged). Few would deny that controversies are a pervasive part of the human condition and exist on virtually every level of human enterprise. Controversies transpire between individuals and among groups, within nations and between nations. Controversies supply the grist necessary for progress by providing challenges and challengers to the status quo. They also create atmospheres where strife and warfare can flourish. A world without controversies would be a peaceful world; but it also would be, by and large, static and prosaic.

The Series' Purpose

The purpose of the Current Controversies series is to explore many of the social, political, and economic controversies dominating the national and international scenes today. Titles selected for inclusion in the series are highly focused and specific. For example, from the larger category of criminal justice, Current Controversies deals with specific topics such as police brutality, gun control, white collar crime, and others. The debates in Current Controversies also are presented in a useful, timeless fashion. Articles and book excerpts included in each title are selected if they contribute valuable, long-range ideas to the overall debate. And wherever possible, current information is enhanced with historical documents and other relevant materials. Thus, while individual titles are current in focus, every effort is made to ensure that they will not become quickly outdated. Books in the Current Controversies series will remain important resources for librarians, teachers, and students for many years.

In addition to keeping the titles focused and specific, great care is taken in the editorial format of each book in the series. Book introductions and chapter prefaces are offered to provide background material for readers. Chapters are organized around several key questions that are answered with diverse opinions representing all points on the political spectrum. Materials in each chapter include opinions in which authors clearly disagree as well as alternative opinions in which authors may agree on a broader issue but disagree on the possible solutions. In this way, the content of each volume in Current Controversies mirrors the mosaic of opinions encountered in society. Readers will quickly realize that there are many viable answers to these complex issues. By questioning each author's conclusions, students and casual readers can begin to develop the critical thinking skills so important to evaluating opinionated material.

Current Controversies is also ideal for controlled research. Each anthology in the series is composed of primary sources taken from a wide gamut of informational categories including periodicals, newspapers, books, U.S. and foreign government documents, and the publications of private and public organizations. Readers will find factual support for reports, debates, and research papers covering all areas of important issues. In addition, an annotated table of contents, an index, a book and periodical bibliography, and a list of organizations to contact are included in each book to expedite further research.

Perhaps more than ever before in history, people are confronted with diverse and contradictory information. During the Persian Gulf War, for example, the public was not only treated to minute-to-minute coverage of the war, it was also inundated with critiques of the coverage and countless analyses of the factors motivating U.S. involvement. Being able to sort through the plethora of opinions accompanying today's major issues, and to draw one's own conclusions, can be a complicated and frustrating struggle. It is the editors' hope that Current Controversies will help readers with this struggle.

Introduction

> *"The health care reform passed by the Obama administration may have ended the current debate about health care legislation, but it certainly has not ended the debate about health care."*

The issue of health care in America has been one of great debate for several decades. Various presidents in the twentieth century made attempts to enact federal health care reform, most of which failed to pass. President Franklin D. Roosevelt tried to enact a publicly funded health care program in 1933, but was opposed by the American Medical Association. President Harry Truman was the first president to propose a national health insurance program, during World War II, but failed to garner the support needed for such a program. President Lyndon B. Johnson enacted the Medicare program in 1965, which provides health insurance coverage to people aged sixty-five and older or those who meet other criteria. President Richard M. Nixon attempted to pass the Comprehensive Health Insurance Act in 1974, which would have mandated that employers purchase health insurance for their employees, but the act did not pass. President Bill Clinton proposed a health care reform package in 1993, but the package failed to pass Congress.

The most significant federal health care reform since the enactment of Medicare occurred on March 23, 2010, when President Barack Obama signed into law the Patient Protection and Affordable Care Act. According to the White House, the key provisions of the act that take effect immediately include the following:

- Small businesses will receive tax credits of up to 35 percent of premiums to make employee coverage more affordable. Beginning in 2014, the tax credit will cover 50 percent of premiums.

- New health plans are prohibited from denying coverage to children with preexisting medical conditions. Beginning in 2014, the prohibition will apply to all persons.

- A temporary high-risk insurance pool will provide affordable insurance to people who are uninsured due to preexisting conditions, until the prohibition takes place.

- Insurance companies are banned from dropping people from health insurance coverage when they get sick.

- New health plans are required to allow young people to remain on their parents' health insurance policy until their twenty-sixth birthday.

- Health insurance companies are prohibited from placing lifetime caps on health insurance coverage and restricting annual limits. Beginning in 2014, all annual limits will be banned.

- New health insurance plans are required to provide free preventative services.[1]

The Congressional Budget Office (CBO) estimates that an additional 32 million people will get coverage under the health care bill, expanding health care coverage to 95 percent of Americans. The CBO estimates that the new health care reform will cut the federal deficit by $130 billion in its first ten years and by $1.2 trillion in its second ten years.[2]

The Patient Protection and Affordable Care Act comes at the end of an extremely contentious yearlong public debate about health care reform, and not everyone is happy about its

1. White House, "Key Provisions of Health Reform That Take Effect Immediately," www.whitehouse.gov.
2. Congressional Budget Office, March 18, 2010. www.cbo.gov.

passage. Many opponents of the act argue that the reform does nothing to control costs. Republican representative from Wisconsin Paul Ryan argues, "A serious fix for what ails health care in America will entail far more than merely tweaking the new law of the land; we will need to repeal the entire faulty architecture of the government behemoth and replace it with real reform."[3] Those in favor of the act argue that the plan will not necessarily have its intended effects without hard work. Jonathan Cohn, author of *Sick: The Untold Story of America's Health Care Crisis—and the People Who Pay the Price*, notes, "Much as the Iraq war wasn't over when American forces conquered Baghdad, so health care reform didn't end when President Obama signed the bill."[4]

Among some of the more contentious parts of the act are those that do not take effect immediately. The act will require most U.S. citizens and residents to have health insurance. Those without coverage will begin paying a tax penalty in 2014, which will reach a full penalty in 2016 of up to $2,085 or 2.5 percent of household income. Many have argued that the mandate to buy insurance by creating a tax penalty is unconstitutional. Constitutional law professor Randy E. Barnett argues, "Never before has a 'tax' penalty been used to mandate, rather than discourage or prohibit, economic activity."[5] Another controversial portion of the act requires employers with more than two hundred employees to provide health insurance and requires those with more than fifty to pay extra taxes or provide health insurance by 2014. Heritage Foundation policy analyst John L. Ligon contends that the employer mandates on medium-size and large businesses will cause

3. Paul Ryan, "Fix Health Reform, Then Repeal It," *New York Times*, March 25, 2010. www.nytimes.com.
4. Jonathan Cohn, "Now Comes the Hard Part," *New York Times*, March 25, 2010. www.nytimes.com.
5. Randy E. Barnett, "The Insurance Mandate in Peril," *Wall Street Journal*, April 29, 2010. http://online.wsj.com.

health insurance premiums to rise, which "will disproportionately affect these medium-size companies as well as smaller companies."[6] Also controversial are the government subsidies provided for individuals to purchase health insurance through state-based American Health Benefit Exchanges and Small Business Health Options Program (SHOP) Exchanges.

The health care reform passed by the Obama administration may have ended the current debate about health care legislation, but it certainly has not ended the debate about health care. By presenting competing views on the current state of the U.S. health care system, governmental involvement in ensuring access to health insurance, a public health insurance option, and other health care reform proposals, *Current Controversies: Health Care* illuminates the debate about health care that has been going on for many decades and is unlikely to cease anytime soon.

6. John L. Ligon, "Obamacare: Impact on Businesses," Heritage Foundation, April 27, 2010. www.heritage.org.

CHAPTER 1

What Is the Current State of the Health Care System in America?

Overview: American Health Care

Public Agenda

Public Agenda is a nonprofit, nonpartisan organization that provides unbiased research in an attempt to bridge the gap between American leaders and what the public really thinks about issues in American life.

The nation's health care system is once again under the microscope as growing numbers of Americans are uninsured, costs keep rising, and the public grows increasingly worried about it.

Health Care Spending

The U.S. spends more money on health care than any other nation. Health care spending will increase to $4.3 trillion by 2017, or $13,000 per person, according to the annual projection by the Centers for Medicare & Medicaid Services. Put another way, the rate of annual growth for health care will be 6.7 percent, which is three times the rate of inflation. Experts attribute the increase to higher demand for care and an aging population.

Yet higher spending on health care does not necessarily correspond to a healthier population, or even that everyone will get care. Some 47 million Americans go without health insurance, according to the Census Bureau, mostly people in jobs that don't offer it as an employee benefit. One-third of adults in the United States are obese, one of the highest rates in the world, according to the National Center for Health Statistics. Children too are increasingly overweight, contributing in part to the unprecedented levels of long-term health conditions like diabetes. And although Americans are indeed living longer than ever, the U.S. has been slipping in international rankings of life expectancy (it's currently at No. 42).

Managed Coverage and Moderating Costs

Countries rich and poor all struggle with how to provide affordable health care for their citizens without breaking the bank. Many countries, such as Canada and Britain, for example, have national health insurance programs, where the government provides health care. But the U.S. health care system is more market-driven, combining both private insurance and government programs.

Most Americans (about six in 10) get their health coverage as an employee benefit. As a result, the number of uninsured people tends to swing up and down with the economy, as employers lay off or cut back in hard times. Low-income people and young adults are most likely to be uninsured. Those without insurance are 25 percent more likely to die during any given year than those with insurance. And of course, even though people with employer-provided insurance only pay a fraction of their health costs, it's far from free—the Kaiser Family Foundation reports the average family premium is more than $12,000 per year, of which employees pay roughly one-quarter.

Higher spending on health care does not necessarily correspond to a healthier population.

The government does play a major role in providing health care, through programs for the elderly (Medicare), the poor (Medicaid) and low-income children, as well as through veterans benefits and insurance for federal employees and their families. In fact, the federal government currently pays for more than 40 percent of the nation's health care bills. The government also provides substantial tax breaks ($225 billion total) for employers who provide insurance.

People who aren't covered by an employer or the government can still buy health coverage from an insurance company on their own—but relatively few do. Individuals end up paying the highest rates, because businesses usually negotiate a cheaper group rate.

Some proposals to rein in health costs include embracing a free-market approach to make the insurance marketplace more competitive and less expensive by using tax credits to encourage more people to buy health insurance on their own instead of receiving it from their employers. Supporters say one reason expenses are rising is that it's hard for most people to tell how much their health care really costs. Most people who have insurance only pay part of the cost through co-pays, deductibles or employee contributions—the insurance company pays the rest, and the patient may or may not ever see a bill. And since different insurance plans negotiate different deals with providers, the bills for two people with the same illness could be quite different. Many experts say that since the patient isn't bearing the real cost, there's no incentive to control costs.

Access to health care and its costs now top Americans' perceptions of the most urgent health problem facing the country today.

Other experts say the only real way to tame health care costs is to do what Canada and many European countries have done by going to a government "single-payer" plan, something that might work like Medicare or Medicaid but would cover everyone. Advocates say countries say this will cut costs because the government could eliminate the inefficiency in our current mixed system and use its enormous purchasing power to get the best deals. Opponents say this would wipe out private insurance and leave employers and patients with less control over their coverage.

In the absence of any national health insurance, some states and municipalities are taking action themselves to provide universal coverage: San Francisco, for example, offers free or subsidized health care to all city adults without insurance. Since 2007, Massachusetts has required residents to have health insurance, with state subsidies available to make it affordable for low-income residents.

Americans' Views on Health Care

On this issue, the attitudes of many Americans are a bundle of contradictions, which is an indication that, on many issues, the public has not yet "worked through" their views. Majorities say the health care system needs to be fundamentally changed, and most say it is the government's responsibility to ensure everyone has adequate health care coverage. But responses vary when faced with the potential costs and trade-offs of a universal health care system.

Access to health care and its costs now top Americans' perceptions of the most urgent health problem facing the country today, a marked change from two decades ago when AIDS ranked first on the list of the nation's health problems, and virtually no one mentioned access or costs.

More than half of Americans say they are dissatisfied with the quality of health care in the U.S. Most say HMOs [health maintenance organizations] and other managed-care programs have decreased the quality of care, and a majority says HMOs do a bad job serving their customers. Yet most Americans belong to managed-care plans, and the vast majority report receiving good or excellent care for themselves and their families.

The American Health Care System Is Long Overdue for Reform

Kathleen Sebelius

Kathleen Sebelius is currently serving as secretary of Health and Human Services.

Health reform constitutes our most important domestic priority and is an integral part of economic recovery. Since 2000, health insurance premiums have almost doubled, growing three times faster than wages. A Kaiser Family Foundation survey found over half of all Americans, insured and uninsured, cut back on health care in the last year due to cost. This means foregone opportunities for chronic disease management and prevention. We will surely pay a price later for this postponed care now. And behind these statistics are stories of struggles for too many American families—unaffordable employer-sponsored insurance premiums of over $12,000 a year on average and rising—competing with education and housing.

As the American economy continues to transform, it is expected that fewer and fewer employers will offer coverage. And we know that during this recession, many people are losing health insurance as they lose their jobs. Even families who do have some coverage are suffering. From 2003 to 2007, the number of "under-insured" families—those who pay for coverage but are unprotected against high costs—rose by 60 percent. Small businesses and their workers are suffering. From 2000 to 2007, the proportion of non-elderly Americans covered by employer-based health insurance fell from 66% to 61%. Much of this decline is attributed to small businesses

Kathleen Sebelius, Testimony of Kathleen Sebelius, "Hearing of the House Energy and Commerce Committee, Health Reform Discussion Draft," U.S. Department of Health and Human Services, June 24, 2009.

dropping coverage. The percentage of small businesses offering coverage dropped from 68% to 59% over the same period, according to a Kaiser Family Foundation survey of small businesses.

We have by far the most expensive health system in the world. We spend 50 percent more per person than the average developed country—spending more on health care than housing or food. And the situation is getting worse. Without reform, according to the Medicare actuaries, we will spend about $4.4 trillion on health care in 2018 and CBO [Congressional Budget Office] estimates that the number of uninsured will grow to 54 million people by 2019. By 2040, health care costs will reach 34 percent of our GDP [gross domestic product] and 72 million Americans will be uninsured.

Savings to Be Gained

As the RAND [Corporation] report documented, we have a system with overutilization, under-utilization, and inconsistent quality. Less than half of our population gets appropriate care at the right time. The payment incentives reward waste, duplication, and lack of coordination. We know that there are substantial savings to be gained just from making our health care system more efficient and responsive.

There are many problems with our health system today.

Rising health costs represent the greatest threat to our long-term economic stability. The CMS [Centers for Medicare and Medicaid Services] Office of the Actuary estimates that by 2018, over one-fifth (20.3 percent) of our economic output will be tied up in the health system, limiting other investments and priorities. Solving this problem is essential to job growth, productivity, and economic mobility. We simply cannot become the nimble economy we need to be without health care reform.

We have certainly received a poor return on all of our spending. In the industrialized world, we have the highest rate of medically preventable deaths and almost 100,000 people die every year from medical errors and poor quality. That's the equivalent of two jumbo jets falling out of the sky every day. Meanwhile, the health status of our citizens declines, with chronic disease accounting for 75 percent of our health care costs and 96 percent of Medicare costs.

Health Information Technology

There are many problems with our health system today. But there is also reason for optimism. In America today, there are already examples of hospitals and providers who are using new technology, cutting costs and improving the quality of care. Two weeks ago, I was in Omaha, Nebraska, at one of the nation's first paperless hospitals and saw firsthand how health information technology can help doctors and patients.

I have spoken to community health center operators from Ohio, Tennessee and Pennsylvania who have outlined how health information technology has helped them save resources and provide better care to their patients. Our challenge now is to take these best practices and spread them across the entire country. But I have every confidence that we can meet this challenge and achieve our goals. And we can do this without adding to the deficit.

Inaction is not an option.

The president is open to good ideas about how we finance health reform. But we will not add to the deficit in the next decade. The president has introduced proposals that will provide nearly $950 billion over 10 years to finance health reform. Much of these resources come from increasing efficiency and wringing waste out of the current system. We are currently paying for strategies that don't work or overpaying for medicines and equipment.

It's time to make better use of these dollars. We know reform can reduce costs for families, businesses and government; protects people's choice of doctors, hospitals and health plans; and assures affordable, quality health care for all Americans.

And as we move forward, we will be guided by a simple principle: protect what works about health care and fix what's broken.

Time for Reform

This is why I share the president's conviction that "health care reform cannot wait, it must not wait, and it will not wait another year." Inaction is not an option. Every delay raises the price tag. The Obama administration is focused on passing health reform legislation that will end the unsustainable status quo and adhere to eight basic principles.

First, we must pass comprehensive reform that makes health care affordable for businesses, government, and families. The high cost of care cripples businesses struggling to provide care to their employees and remain competitive. It drives budget deficits and weakens our economy.

Second, we must protect families from bankruptcy or debt because of health care costs. Today, many patients worry more about being able to pay their medical bills than worry about restoring their health. They have reason to be concerned. In America, half of all personal bankruptcies are related to medical expenses. It's time to fix a system that has plunged millions into debt, simply because they have fallen ill.

Third, we must assure affordable, quality health coverage for all Americans. The large number of uninsured Americans impose a hidden tax on other citizens as premiums go up and leave too many Americans wondering where they will turn if they get sick. The lack of continuity of coverage affects individual health and our national health status. Lack of insurance and interruptions in coverage take their toll by reducing our ability to effectively address chronic disease and improve prevention. They affect our ability to control the spread of infectious diseases. And they affect our productivity. According to the Institute of Medicine, employers lose billions of dollars of productivity each year from uninsured workers with unnecessarily prolonged and untreated illnesses.

No one is immune from the risk of becoming uninsured. No American is guaranteed that they will have the same health insurance benefits next week that they have today. In its effects on the health care system, on the health of our society, and on our economy, the risk of being uninsured affects us all.

It's time to fix a system that has plunged millions into debt, simply because they have fallen ill.

Fourth, we will guarantee choice of doctors and health plans. No American should be forced to give up the doctor they trust or the health plan they like. If you like your current health care, you can keep it. And if you like your doctor, you need to be able to keep that doctor.

Fifth, we will make sure that Americans who lose or change jobs can keep their coverage. Americans should not lose their health care simply because they have lost their jobs or want to pursue better opportunities.

Sixth, we must end barriers to coverage including prohibitive insurance premiums for people with preexisting medical conditions. In Kansas and across the country, I have heard painful stories from families who have been denied basic care or offered insurance at astronomical rates because of preexisting conditions from cancer to childhood ear infections. Insurance companies should no longer have the right to pick and choose. We will not allow these companies to insure only the healthy, leaving families stranded in planning for their health care.

Seventh, we must make important investments in prevention and wellness. The old adage is true—an ounce of prevention truly is worth a pound of cure. But for too long, we've sunk all our resources into cures and shortchanged prevention. Preventing disease and controlling its effects over time need to be the foundation of our health care system.

And finally, any reform legislation must take steps to improve patient safety and the quality of care in America. Our country is home to some of the finest, most advanced medicine in the world. But today, health care-associated infections—infections caught in hospitals or other settings—are one of the leading causes of death in our nation. More Americans die each year as a result of these and other quality deficiencies than die from car accidents, breast cancer, or AIDS. These numbers are not acceptable for the world's richest nation. Despite the best efforts of business purchasers and private quality improvement initiatives and the development of standards, both government and private, recent reports indicate that the quality of care has actually declined in recent years. We will not be able to achieve the quality we need without the major reforms the president seeks. It will take a comprehensive approach to provide the leverage needed to improve care.

The Quality of U.S. Health Care Is Better than Studies Say

James Peron

James Peron is the president of Laissez Faire Books and editor of its magazine, Laissez Faire!

It is curious that the United States ranked below Europe in the World Health Organization's [WHO's] 2000 World Health Report, which rated 191 countries' medical systems. In his documentary *Sicko*, socialist Michael Moore makes hay out of the fact that the United States placed 37th, behind even Morocco, Cyprus, and Costa Rica. This ranking is used to "prove" that state-controlled health care is superior to the "free market."

This ranking is curious because the actual life expectancy of the average American differs very little from that of the average European. At birth, average life expectancy in the European Union is 78.7. For the average American it is 78. And this doesn't adjust for factors that can affect the averages which are unrelated to health care, such as lifestyle choices, accident rates, crime rates, and immigration. Health isn't entirely about longevity but it certainly is a major component.

The Measures of Health Care

What is not mentioned by Moore, or others citing the WHO report, are the measures being used to rate the various countries and who is doing the measuring. There are many ways to nudge ratings in one direction or another that are not directly related to the actual item being measured.

James Peron, "Ranking the U.S. Health-Care System," *Freeman*, vol. 57, no. 9, November 2007. Copyright © 2007 Foundation for Economic Education, Incorporated. www.fee.org. All rights reserved. Reproduced by permission.

For instance, one might produce a study on transportation. The purpose of transportation is to get people from where they are to where they wish to be. You might rate how quickly people can move, how cheaply they can move relative to their income, how conveniently they can move, and how free they are to move.

The actual life expectancy of the average American differs very little from that of the average European.

You would think the United States would rate high in such a study. Americans tend to be wealthier than the rest of the world. There is widespread ownership of cars. Gasoline prices are lower than in most other countries. On average, the typical American can travel quicker, cheaper, and more conveniently than people in most parts of the world. But what if this index included other factors as well? For instance, if a major component was the percentage of commuters who use public transportation, that would push the United States far down in the ranking. A larger percentage of the people in other countries have no other option but public transportation.

In 2000, when the report was issued, WHO was run by Gro Harlem Brundtland, a former prime minister of Norway and a socialist. She doesn't think the results of a health system alone are important. Rather, she wants to know if the system is "fair." In introducing the WHO report she wrote that while the goal of a health system "is to improve and protect health," it also has "other intrinsic goals [that] are concerned with fairness in the way people pay for health care." She is clear about the ideological factors she thinks are important: "Where health and responsiveness are concerned, achieving a high average level is not good enough: The goals of a health system must also include reducing inequalities, in ways that improve the situation of the worst-off. In this report attainment in relation to these goals provides the basis for measuring the performance of health systems."

The Preference for Socialized Medicine

True to her ideological roots, Brundtland prefers socialized medicine over private care. Drawing her first conclusion about what makes a good medical system, she declares: "Ultimate responsibility for the performance of a country's health system lies with government. The careful and responsible management of the well-being of the population—stewardship—is the very essence of good government. The health of people is always a national priority: government responsibility for it is continuous and permanent."

The American system loses points because it doesn't provide socialized medicine.

One WHO discussion paper states, regarding "fairness" in financing, "we consider only the distribution, not the level, as there is no consensus on what the level of health spending should be." Equal results, not necessarily good results, are the focus.

When Moore or others refer to the WHO index as proof that private health care doesn't work, they aren't being totally honest because they fail to disclose that the index lowers the scores of systems that don't satisfy socialist presumptions.

The *New York Times* in August [2007] editorialized that American health care "lags well behind other advanced nations." The newspaper relied in part on the WHO rankings as proof. For the rest, it relied on a more recent study by the Commonwealth Fund. But that study, which compared the United States to five other wealthy countries, has weaknesses similar to the WHO study.

The Commonwealth Fund marked down the United States partly because "all other major industrialized nations provide universal health coverage, and most of them have comprehensive benefits packages with no cost-sharing by the patients." Again the American system loses points because it doesn't provide socialized medicine. And the *Times* neglected to note that "no cost-sharing" means the people have paid through taxes whether they receive the care or not.

Waiting Time for Treatment

The United States also was penalized because seeing a physician for non-emergency reasons is harder to do on nights and weekends than in the other five nations. The Fund said "many report having to wait six days or more for an appointment with their own doctors."

The survey didn't look at the treatment of serious conditions. Waiting weeks or months for chemotherapy is not held against a health care system, but waiting a few days to have a checkup is. Waiting time for "elective" surgery is counted (the United States was a close second to Germany), but waiting time for nonelective, serious surgery did not count, though that is precisely where socialist systems do the worst.

This issue is not unknown to the Commonwealth Fund. In 1999 it published *The Elderly's Experiences with Health Care in Five Nations*, which found significant delays for "serious surgery." Only 4 percent of the American seniors reported long waits for serious surgery. The rate was 11 percent in Canada and 13 percent in Britain. For nonserious surgery the differences were more obvious: 7 percent in the United States, 40 percent in Canada, and 51 percent in Britain.

Patient Perceptions

In the latest survey, the United States came in dead last for health "safety," but many of the scores were only a few points apart. For instance, 15 percent of American patients said they "believed a medical mistake" had been made in their treatment within the last two years. Notice this is merely patient perception and nothing objective. But the best score was in Britain, where 12 percent said this.

The United States is also marked down because 23 percent of patients report delayed or incorrect results on medical tests they took. That is far worse than the best country, Germany, at 9 percent. But what constitutes a delay? If a result is expected in a week but takes two, that is a delay. But if it is expected in three weeks and arrives then, that isn't a delay. Thus what constitutes a delay depends on expectations, leading to counterintuitive results.

The United States also lost credit because fewer Americans report having a regular doctor for five years or more. But Americans are more mobile than many other people. CNN reports that Americans move every five years on average. In comparison, Britain has a moving rate of 10 percent a year, or an average of once a decade. And 60 percent of those move about three miles.

Americans are also freer to change doctors if they wish. Britain requires patients to sign up with physicians, and once they do so, they are pretty much stuck unless they want to end up on the waiting list of another physician. Patients often have to wait to get on the books of a physician and only then can they be treated; that is, they wait to get on a wait list. This is true even for heart transplants. The inevitable waiting is a disincentive to change doctors.

Another measure used by the Commonwealth Fund is centralization of medical records. If a country has a system that allows doctors anywhere to tap into the patients' records, it is rated higher. The United States has no centralized database and so is rated lower. Many Americans may prefer to have their records private and dispersed. When the [President Bill] Clinton plan was proposed in 1993, one of the rallying points that helped defeat it was the centralization of health records.

Out-of-pocket expenses were counted against a system as well. In socialized health care these expenses are zero or very low but are replaced with taxes. Taxes, however, don't lower a country's score because the care "is free."

One could easily design a survey that would rank American health care high and other nations low.

Countries were also judged on the number of patient complaints. But different cultures have different attitudes toward complaining. Jeremy Laurance wrote in the *Belfast Telegraph* recently that the National Health Service needs "a healthy dose of American belligerence."

An Irrelevant Ranking

Finally, the United States is ranked last among the six nations surveyed in infant mortality. What is not discussed is that nations define infant mortality differently. Any infant, regardless of size or weight or premature status, who shows sign of life is counted as a live birth in the United States. Germany, which ranks number one in the Commonwealth Fund survey, doesn't count as a live birth any infant with a birth weight under 500 grams (one pound). How valuable is a comparison under those circumstances?

One could easily design a survey that would rank American health care high and other nations low. But this does not mean the American system is what it should be. Its successes and innovation can be attributed to the vestiges of freedom, but government has saddled the system with so much intervention that it is far from market oriented. Instead of worrying about irrelevant international rankings, we should be working toward freeing the medical market.

The Quality of U.S. Health Care Is Not the Best in the World

Elizabeth Docteur and Robert A. Berenson

Elizabeth Docteur is vice president of the Center for Studying Health System Change. Robert A. Berenson is a senior fellow at the Urban Institute and an adjunct professor at the University of North Carolina Gillings School of Global Public Health and the Fuqua School of Business at Duke University.

There is a perception among many Americans that despite coverage, cost and other problems in the health care system, the quality of health care in the United States is better than it is anywhere else in the world and might be threatened by health reform. In fact, 55 percent of Americans surveyed last year [2008] said U.S. patients receive better quality of care than do those in other nations, even though only 45 percent said they thought the United States had the world's best health care system. And while Americans overwhelmingly support government action to increase coverage and reduce the costs of health care, a recent poll found that 63 percent worry that the quality of their own care would get worse if the government ensured health care for all. Another poll found that as many as 81 percent of Americans have such concerns.

Quality and Reform

Participants in the current reform debate refer to the relative quality of U.S. health care as providing support for their views, and perceptions of health care quality—what it is and where it can be found—are often at the heart of disagreements over

Elizabeth Docteur and Robert A. Berenson, "How Does the Quality of U.S. Health Care Compare Internationally?" Health Policy Center, Urban Institute, August 2009, pp. 1–7, 9. Copyright © 2009 Urban Institute. Reproduced by permission.

what form of health reform the country should adopt. But hard facts to support claims are often missing, and it is clear that quality of care experts, policy makers, health care providers and the general public all have different ideas as to which aspects of health care signify its quality and which ones are most important.

This brief brings together available evidence on how quality of care in the United States compares to that of other countries and comments on the implications of the evidence for the health reform debate. By exploring how the quality of our care compares internationally, we can address the underlying attitudes and concerns that people have about health reform. For example, if claims that the United States has the best quality of care in the world—overall or in particular respects—were well supported by the evidence, it would caution us against adopting forms of health reform that threaten those attributes of our health system responsible for this standing. But if quality of care is not remarkable—or may be even lagging—there should be less reluctance to change. In addition, a more explicit need for health reform to address quality improvement would appear warranted.

The Definition of Quality

A number of definitions of health care quality have been put forward over the years. The U.S. Institute of Medicine's definition, which has grounded expert work in the United States and elsewhere, describes quality as "the degree to which health services for individuals and populations increase the likelihood of desired health outcomes and are consistent with current professional knowledge." A similar definition is used by the U.S. Agency for Healthcare Research and Quality: "Quality health care means doing the right thing at the right time in the right way for the right person and having the best results possible." Both definitions refer to characteristics of health care that are increasingly referred to as "technical" or "clinical" quality or "effectiveness."

In the context of efforts to assess health system performance, the term "quality" is often used to encompass a range of desirable or positive attributes of health care and the overall performance of health care systems. A review of eight country-specific and internationally developed frameworks for evaluating health systems found a great deal of commonality in how performance has been conceptualized. In addition to effectiveness, the researchers identified 14 other dimensions of the performance of health care systems: acceptability, accessibility, appropriateness, care environment and amenities, competence or capability, continuity, expenditure or cost, efficiency, equity, governance, patient-centeredness (-focus) or responsiveness, safety, sustainability, and timeliness.

By exploring how the quality of our care compares internationally, we can address the underlying attitudes and concerns that people have about health reform.

Many of these performance dimensions might reasonably be considered to be attributes of high-quality care (e.g., appropriateness, competence, timeliness). Those in a second group (e.g., cost, governance, sustainability) are readily observed as separate performance concerns. Reasonable people might have different views on whether others (e.g., accessibility, acceptability, responsiveness) are dimensions of quality or closely related concepts, and indeed these are treated in different ways in the frameworks reviewed. Accessibility is particularly difficult to disentangle from considerations of health care quality in that it is a prerequisite to receipt of quality health care. Availability of providers and services, coverage, benefits and affordability all come into play as potential explanations for different user experiences with the health care system and the outcomes attained. Finally, (technical) efficiency is a function of the quality and quantity of services produced at a given cost. Efficiency, or value for money, is a performance consideration of great interest to public authorities and purchasers, although only modest headway in measuring efficiency in health care has been made to date, reflecting limitations in the capacity to measure the quality of health care.

It is evident from the U.S. reform debates that popular conceptions of what constitutes good quality health care encompass a range of dimensions. Although obviously high quality implies superior health outcomes, other attributes considered indicative of quality appear to underlie popular expressions of U.S. health care superiority, including a belief that Americans with good insurance coverage uniquely benefit from prompt availability and accessibility of cutting-edge medical procedures, medicines, and devices, as well as highly educated and well-trained health care professionals, who know and consistently do what is best for their patients. On the other hand, those who assert that we have inferior quality of care point to our relatively poor population health status and factors such as barriers to access for those without adequate insurance coverage or limited health plan provider networks and insufficient coordination among providers in the fragmented health care delivery system.

All of these aspects of quality and broader health system performance are important and legitimate considerations; therefore, we cast a relatively wide net in this brief. Specifically, we focus on effectiveness (or "technical" or "clinical" quality) and consider additional dimensions of quality or health system performance that are most closely related: appropriateness, safety, accessibility, acceptability, and responsiveness.

Cross-Country Comparisons

To make an informed assessment about the quality of care in one health system versus another, it is important to look at a wide range of indicators. Because health care involves a complex array of activities, and because there are many holes in our knowledge of the relative quality in many areas, it is impossible to use a single measure as a meaningful proxy. Measures that reflect multiple dimensions of quality have a certain appeal as performance indicators for policy makers, although more specific or narrow measures have the advantage of being more actionable for administrators and clinicians. And even with a broad set of comparative measures, people may differ on which measures are most important, for example, those focusing on the level of typical or average care for common conditions versus the care available for unusual, life-threatening conditions.

The evidentiary basis for cross-country comparisons of quality could be strengthened by additional studies and improvements in methods and data. Nonetheless, a number of comparative studies on the quality of care have been published. Below we review some of the key findings from recent research that provide insight on how the quality of care in the United States compares to the quality of care in other nations. We explore quality as assessed by measures based upon population health status, measures of processes and outcomes of care for particular conditions, measures of patient safety, and indicators based on patients' experience with health services. In each area, we put forward the evidence we could find on how the attribute in question stacks up (or fails to do so).

Life Expectancy and Mortality

While U.S. life expectancy is at or below the average in comparison with that of other developed countries, findings from research that has adjusted mortality to account for deaths not related to health care (so-called amenable mortality) show the United States to be among the worst performers.

The United States is not among top performers in terms of life expectancy, an indicator influenced by factors outside the health system in addition to health care. We rank among the lower third of developed countries in life expectancy at birth. Life expectancy at age 65 may be a better indicator of U.S. health care performance because all older Americans have reasonably good insurance coverage through Medicare. U.S. life expectancy for both men and women at age 65 is above the Organisation for Economic Co-operation and Development (OECD) average, but below what the top countries have achieved, particularly for women.

To make an informed assessment about the quality of care in one health system versus another, it is important to look at a wide range of indicators.

Among 19 countries included in a recent study of amenable mortality, the United States had the highest rate of deaths from conditions that could have been prevented or treated successfully. The extent to which differences across countries in the prevalence of particular conditions may explain the poor U.S. showing in the recent study is unknown, although studies in which it was possible to adjust for such differences found that the greatest part of regional differences in mortality for certain conditions were explained by differences in disease prevalence. A recent study comparing the United States and 10 European countries found that the United States had a much higher prevalence of nine of 10 conditions, including cancer, heart disease, and stroke, in its population over age 50. However, it is unlikely that relative differences across countries in the prevalence of disease changed during the five years that had passed since an earlier study by the same authors using the same methodology, in which the U.S. health system ranked somewhat better (16 of 19) among its peers in minimizing amenable mortality. In the years between the two studies, there was an average reduction in amenable mortality for men of 17 percent across all countries included in the study, compared with only a 4 percent reduction in the rate of amenable mortality for men in the United States.

Studies of Processes and Outcomes of Care

Measures specifically designed to assess technical/clinical quality of care focus on health services and health outcomes, such as five-year survival rates for individuals with particular conditions. Such measures are less sensitive to differences across countries in disease prevalence.

> *Among 19 countries included in a recent study of amenable mortality, the United States had the highest rate of deaths from conditions that could have been prevented or treated successfully.*

Below we review available evidence on U.S. quality of care in a variety of clinical areas, in comparison with other countries. The overall evidence is mixed, indicating that the United States has neither the best nor the worst quality of health care for particular conditions among developed countries. In certain cases where U.S. quality appears low relative to that of other countries—in the areas of prevention and care for chronic conditions, for example—access barriers experienced by the uninsured and the underinsured may contribute to the results seen.

Quality of Preventive Care

The evidence on how the United States compares to other developed countries in terms of the quality of its preventive care is quite mixed.

In a report that summarized survey research comparing quality of care in five countries, [Karen] Davis et al. concluded that the United States had relatively high-quality preventive care. 85 percent of American women reported having had a Pap smear within the last two years and 84 percent of American women age 50 to 64 reported having received a mammogram within the last two years, the highest shares among the countries included in the survey. Perhaps reflecting differences in data sources, the OECD found that the United States had above-average mammography rates (61 percent U.S. versus 55 percent OECD), although was far below the best performers (82–98 percent in four countries). However, the United States had the highest cervical cancer screening rate (83 percent) among 22 countries reporting data to OECD.

Among 30 OECD countries, the United States had above-average rates of flu vaccination for senior citizens (65 percent U.S. versus 55 percent OECD average and 80 percent in top-performing Australia). However, childhood vaccination rates were below the OECD average. The U.S. pertussis vaccination rate stood at 86 percent in 2005; only Austria and Canada reported lower rates. Even with a 92 percent childhood measles vaccination, the United States came in below average in a field where one-third of OECD countries have rates above 95 percent.

Among 30 OECD countries, the United States ranked below average in adult asthma care.

Quality of Care for Chronic Conditions

Findings on the quality of U.S. care for several chronic conditions also provide a mixed picture.

Among 30 OECD countries, the United States ranked below average in adult asthma care. Adult hospital admission rates for asthma, an indicator of inadequate care for the condition, were second highest among 17 countries reporting (12 per 10,000 U.S. versus 5.8 OECD average) and U.S. asthma mortality, double the OECD average rate, was fifth highest among 25 countries reporting.

A handful of studies undertaken in the 1990s have compared outcomes for U.S. and Canadian patients with end-stage renal disease and found that Canadians have longer survival times while in hemodialysis or peritoneal dialysis programs, and after receipt of kidney transplant, even when extensive adjustment for comorbidity is done.

A survey of patients in six countries found that more than half of U.S. diabetics had received four recommended services, a rate comparable to the UK [United Kingdom] and Germany, and higher than the rate seen in Australia, Canada and New Zealand. The same survey found that 85 percent of U.S. hypertension patients reported having received two recommended tests, a rate identical to Canada and exceeded only by Germany (91 percent). . . .

Quality of Cancer Care

While interpreting the available evidence is challenging in the light of different screening protocols across countries, it does suggest that the United States as one of several world leaders in providing high-quality cancer care.

A study by [Gemma] Gatta and colleagues looked at five-year cancer survival rates for the United States and 17 European countries. The United States had the highest survival rates for cancer of the colon, rectum, lung, breast, and prostate. U.S. survival rates were also among the highest for melanoma (fourth), uterine (second) and ovarian (fifth) cancer, cervical cancer (sixth), Hodgkin's disease (third) and non-Hodgkin's lymphoma (fourth). The United States was ninth in survival of stomach cancer. Although average survival differences between the United States and Europe as a whole were in some cases large, the difference between the United States and the other countries with relatively high five-year survival rates were generally small (approximately 3 to 4 percent for many cancers) and (due to small sample sizes) usually not statistically significant. The study also looked at cross-country differences by population group, finding that survival rates for colon, breast and uterine cancer were similar in the United

States and Europe for patients under 45 years, but were much better in the United States for patients age 65 or older at diagnosis. In the case of stomach cancer, the U.S. survival rate for patients under age 45 was below those of many European nations, but similar among the older patients. Other studies have also found that U.S. survival rates for certain cancers, particularly prostate cancer, are among the best. Among 30 OECD countries, the United States had one of the best five-year survival rates for patients with breast or colorectal cancer.

Survival and Screening

There is an important link between survival rates and screening rates for many cancers (e.g., melanoma, prostate cancer, breast cancer, colorectal cancer). Many cancers are more amenable to treatment when caught early. But it is also true that in countries with higher screening, more cancers will be diagnosed early, and survival rates in those countries will be higher simply because there are more patients in the denominator with less advanced disease. Thus, Gatta et al. found that those countries with the highest breast cancer incidence rate (share of population newly diagnosed with the disease in a given year) also had the highest survival rates.

Among 30 OECD countries, the United States had one of the best five-year survival rates for patients with breast or colorectal cancer.

Differing national commitments to screening becomes an issue, particularly, in the case of prostate cancer, where U.S. incidence rates are double those of Europe because aggressive screening uncovers cancers at a very early stage. The implications for quality are complicated, in that cancer detection has instigated more treatments with serious risk of quality of life deterioration for a condition that is very slow to develop. In 2008, the U.S. Preventive Services Task Force updated its screening advice, recommending that known risks of screening outweigh potential benefits for older men, and that informed patient preferences should serve as a determinant of appropriate care in younger men. Other countries, such as Denmark, had recommended against widespread use of the test as early as 1990.

Differences across countries in access to diagnostic and treatment services explain most of the observed differences in cancer survival rates. Better survival rates are associated with higher national income levels, higher levels of expenditure on health, and higher investment in health technology, as proxied by indicators such as the rate of CT scanners per person. The relationship between cancer survival and level of expenditure on diagnosis and treatment has yet to be fully explored, due to data limitations, although some cross-country differences in expenditure have been documented. Using an approach to assess relative spending across nations with different income levels, OECD found that the United States spent between 41 and 62 percent of its per capita GDP [gross domestic product] on the first six months of breast cancer treatment following diagnosis for each patient, while Canada and France spent about one-third of their respective per capita GDPs for treatment during the initial phase. . . .

Taken collectively, the findings from international studies of health care quality do not in and of themselves provide a definitive answer to the question of how the United States compares in terms of the quality of its health care. While the evidence base is incomplete and suffers from other limitations, it does not provide support for the oft-repeated claim that the "U.S. health care is the best in the world." In fact, there is no hard evidence that identifies particular areas in which U.S. health care quality is truly exceptional.

U.S. Health Care Costs Are Excessive Because of Overtreatment

Shannon Brownlee

Shannon Brownlee is a senior research fellow in the Economic Growth Program at the New America Foundation and the author of Overtreated: Why Too Much Medicine Is Making Us Sicker and Poorer.

Sandy and Charlie Murphy never imagined that paying for health care could put everything they owned at risk.

The High Cost of Health Care

In 2002 the Murphys and their two sons were living a comfortable middle-class life in Scottsdale, Arizona, where Charlie, now 59, worked as a manager for Charles Schwab and where Sandy, now 60, was a part-time child advocate for the state. Then, in rapid succession, Charlie got laid off; Sandy quit to care for a son with health problems; Charlie discovered that his new employer set a $100,000 cap on lifetime medical-claim payments, necessitating a secondary policy; and the Murphys found themselves struggling to pay for health care. In 2006 their medical costs came to $25,000, most of it to cover insurance premiums—more than their annual mortgage payments.

Why does basic health care cost so much? That's a question you won't hear much in the news, despite the fact that the topic of health care is front and center in this year's [2008's] presidential race. The issue of cost has understandably taken a backseat to our concerns about the 47 million

Americans who have no health insurance. Millions more, like the Murphys, are underinsured—covered so thinly that a single catastrophic illness could wipe them out financially. Even Americans who are fully insured by an employer or Medicare are paying more out of pocket, largely because medical costs are skyrocketing. According to the Congressional Budget Office, in the past 30 years health care spending has risen 2 percent faster annually than the rest of the economy. In 2007 the total U.S. health care bill came to $2.3 trillion—more than we spent last year on food.

In the past 30 years health care spending has risen 2 percent faster annually than the rest of the economy.

What do we get for all that money? Politicians are constantly telling us we have the best health care in the world, but that's simply not the case. By every conceivable measure, the health of Americans lags behind the health of citizens in other developed countries. Our life expectancy is shorter than that of citizens in Canada, Japan, and all but one Western European country. We rank 43rd in the world in infant-mortality rates, behind Cuba, the Czech Republic, and the United Kingdom [UK]. We are no less disabled by disease than citizens of most developed nations, and our medical care is, with few exceptions, no better at helping us survive specific diseases. For instance, the mortality rate from prostate cancer in the United Kingdom is virtually the same as it is in the United States, despite the fact that the disease is treated far less aggressively in the UK.

The Conventional Beliefs About High Cost

Why, then, is our health care so astronomically expensive? Let's look at some of the conventional beliefs.

- *We don't ration care.* Unlike citizens in the UK and Canada, we don't have to wait weeks for elective surgery or an MRI [magnetic resonance imaging]. But when researchers from the Johns Hopkins Bloomberg School of Public Health looked at the 15 procedures and tests that account for the majority of waiting lists in other countries, they found that they amounted to just 3 percent of costs in the United States, not nearly enough to explain the huge difference in spending.

- *Malpractice is the culprit.* Doctors say their worries about lawsuits drive them to order costly tests and procedures that their patients do not actually need. Malpractice reform will help save money, but not as much as some people believe. The Congressional Budget Office estimates that while tort reforms could lower malpractice insurance premiums for physicians by as much as 25 to 30 percent, the overall savings to our health care system would be a minuscule one-half percent.

- *Inefficient insurance companies are to blame.* We devote nearly a third of our health care dollars to administrative costs—paper pushing, in effect. (Canada's single-payer system, by contrast, is a model of efficiency, spending only about 16 percent of its health care dollars on administrative overhead.) If we could be as efficient as Canada, we could save $360 billion each year. That's a lot of money, but it's only about one-seventh of our total health care spending.

- *Consumers aren't shopping wisely.* The moral-hazard argument says that because people don't pay out of pocket, they use more expensive health care than necessary. Moral hazard says we go to the doctor when we don't really need to; we insist on getting a CT [computed tomography] scan for a twisted ankle when ice and an Ace bandage will do. Experts will tell you that as many as one in four doctor's office visits are "social calls," and nearly half of emergency room visits are for care that could have been handled in a nonemergency setting. But even this argument doesn't explain why health care costs so much. That's because 20 percent of patients account for 80 percent of spending, and that 20 percent is made up mostly of the chronically ill. These patients are often sick with multiple conditions—such as diabetes, heart disease, and high blood pressure—and more than half of the money we devote to caring for them is spent when they are in the hospital. People who are sick enough to be hospitalized are generally too ill to be insisting on certain tests or procedures.

Indeed, perhaps the most significant reason Americans are drowning in health care debt may shock you: Americans are getting far too much *unnecessary* care. Of our total $2.3 trillion health care bill last year [2007], a whopping $500 billion to $700 billion was spent on treatments, tests, and hospitalizations that did nothing to improve our health. Even worse, new evidence suggests that too much health care may actually be killing us. According to estimates by Elliott Fisher, M.D., a noted Dartmouth researcher, unnecessary care leads to the deaths of as many as 30,000 Medicare recipients annually.

The Geography of Health Care

For many Americans the idea that doctors are giving us care we don't need—and that may actually be harming us—may seem hard to believe. All too often, our interactions with the health care system make us feel that far from getting too much care, we're getting barely enough. We wait weeks for an appointment, we're rushed through the visit in ten minutes, and when we go to fill the prescription the doctor wrote, we're told our insurance company won't pay for it.

Indeed, one recent study found that due to inefficiencies and the lack of clear standards, patients had just a 50–50 chance of receiving flu shots, aspirin or beta-blockers (for those who had had a heart attack), antibiotics (for those with pneumonia), and other treatments that have been shown to improve health.

At the same time, a mountain of evidence suggests we also are getting care we don't need. To understand the reasons, it helps to take a look at studies pioneered nearly 40 years ago by John E. Wennberg, M.D., director emeritus of Dartmouth's Institute for Health Policy and Clinical Practice. As a young researcher at the University of Vermont, Wennberg discovered that there appeared to be little connection between the availability of medical services, the care that people needed, and what they actually got. For example, in Middlebury [Vermont], a small town south of Burlington, fewer than 10 percent of children under the age of 16 had their tonsils removed. In Morrisville, about a two-hour drive away, nearly 70 percent of children had the procedure. Middlebury wasn't suffering from a shortage of doctors or hospital beds, and their children weren't getting fewer sore throats than the children of Morrisville. It turned out that the Morrisville doctors simply believed a more aggressive approach was best, even though there was no scientific evidence to support that belief. Once Wennberg pointed that out to the Morrisville doctors, they began doing fewer tonsillectomies.

Americans are getting far too much unnecessary *care.*

Since then, researchers at Dartmouth and other academic institutions have continued to find wide discrepancies in how much care patients receive in different parts of the country— and the differences can be stunning. For example, if you are a Medicare recipient and you have a heart attack in a region where doctors practice less aggressive care, like Salt Lake City [Utah], your care will cost Medicare about $23,500 over the course of a year. But if you have your heart attack in a place like Los Angeles, the bill will be closer to $30,000.

The wide gulf in spending between the two cities is not because of different prices. Sure, everything costs a bit more in Los Angeles, including nurses' salaries and the laundering of hospital linens, but not enough to account for the extra amount Medicare pays for a heart attack. The reason the same patient's care costs more there than in Salt Lake City is that doctors and hospitals in Los Angeles tend to give their patients more tests, procedures, and surgeries, and their patients tend to spend more days in the hospital.

The Harms of Overtreatment

But here's the important part. All that extra care in L.A. doesn't lead to better outcomes. As it turns out, heart attack patients who receive the most care actually die at slightly *higher* rates than those who receive less care.

How can more health care be harmful? Just ask Susan Urquhart, 66, an Ann Arbor, Michigan, woman who underwent a hysterectomy she now says was "the worst decision I've ever made in my life." For several years her gynecologist had been urging her to undergo the procedure to treat uterine fibroid tumors, benign growths that can sometimes cause heavy bleeding.

Unnecessary hysterectomies are but one example of how overtreatment can do more harm than good.

"I had heavy bleeding—I'd had it for years," says Urquhart. "But it wasn't interfering with my life." Even so, her gynecologist warned her that the fibroids were growing and said that the best treatment was to remove Urquhart's uterus and ovaries. Despite Urquhart's misgivings about undergoing a surgery for symptoms that did not seem terribly troublesome, she finally consented.

Within weeks after the procedure, she discovered that the side effects of the surgery were far worse than the symptoms caused by her fibroids. Plunged instantly into menopause by the removal of her ovaries, Urquhart had trouble sleeping and began suffering hot flashes and drenching night sweats. Next, she began having trouble with bladder control, a common symptom among women who undergo a hysterectomy. And then her sex drive evaporated. Worst of all, Urquhart's procedure may not have been necessary in the first place. In one recent study, a panel of gynecologists reviewed the records of 497 women who were told to have a hysterectomy. In 367 cases—70 percent—the panel found that the surgery was not needed. And recommendations, in force since the early 1990s, that gynecologists try less invasive treatments first have had little effect on the number of surgeries being performed around the country. To this day, according to Ernst G. Bartsich, M.D., clinical associate professor of obstetrics and gynecology at Weill Cornell Medical College in Manhattan, one in three women has had a hysterectomy by age 60, and one in two by age 65.

Unnecessary hysterectomies are but one example of how overtreatment can do more harm than good. Patients undergo back surgery for pain in the absence of evidence that the surgery works. They contract lethal infections while in the hospital for elective procedures. They suffer strokes when they undergo a surgery that, ironically, is intended to prevent stroke. And each year they undergo millions of tests—MRIs, CT scans, blood tests—that do little to help doctors diagnose disease.

The Reasons for Overtreatment

Many physicians believe that demanding patients are the reason they are delivering so much unnecessary care. Patients insist on getting a prescription for a drug they saw advertised on TV, or on getting an unnecessary and pricey imaging test, such as a CT scan. Doctors comply for fear the patient will leave them for another physician, or because explaining why a drug or a test is unnecessary takes too much time. As one pediatric specialist told me, he'd rather send a child for an unnecessary imaging scan than fight with the kid's parents, who will only think he's incompetent because they *know* their child needs a scan.

Other doctors insist that malpractice suits are the culprit when it comes to rising costs. Though malpractice insurance premiums and payouts constitute only a tiny fraction of our national health care bill, the fear of being sued causes physicians to order unnecessary tests, send patients to specialists, and sometimes even do needless procedures.

Why? Because doctors believe patients will be less likely to go to a lawyer if they think the doctor did everything possible—even when doing so doesn't help the patient or causes harm, as in Susan Urquhart's case. Statistics back this up. The top reason for malpractice payouts involves the failure on the doctor's part to diagnose a disease.

Health care providers have every incentive to give patients more care, not better care.

Online and in person, doctors talk openly about this defensive medicine. "We practice defensive medicine so often, every day, all the time, we aren't even aware we are doing it," says Robert P. Lindeman, M.D., a Natick, Massachusetts, pediatrician.

Shawn D. Newlands, M.D., a professor of otolaryngology [the study of ear, nose, and throat] at the University of Texas Medical Branch in Galveston, says, "You have a patient who comes in with hearing loss. It might be an acoustic neuroma, a very rare [slow-growing] tumor." Some doctors order an MRI for every patient who walks in the door complaining of hearing loss, says Newlands. But a more rational approach is to explain to the patient that there is only a small chance of a tumor. The doctor should say, "Let's check your hearing in six months." But many doctors don't do that, says Newlands, because they worry the patient will go to a physician down the street, who will find a tumor, and the patient will turn around and sue the doctor who suggested waiting. He says, "It's cheaper for the doctor to abuse the system and order an MRI for every patient with hearing loss."

Two other hidden forces are pushing overtreatment. One is the local supply of medical resources. In many parts of the country there are more specialists and more hospital beds than necessary, and the doctors in those regions tend to practice more aggressive care, hospitalizing patients unnecessarily and referring their patients to other specialists, who then perform more unneeded procedures and tests. The other hidden spur toward overtreatment occurs in the way our health care system is set up. Sometimes, providers deliver unneeded care because they get paid more when they do more. Most of our caregivers are still paid through a system known as fee for service. They are reimbursed for each office visit, each day a patient spends in the hospital, and each test or surgery performed. This means that health care providers have every incentive to give patients more care, not better care.

It is essential that we gather better scientific evidence for what works in medicine, what doesn't, and for which patients—and get the word out to doctors.

All too often—but what's not well known by the public—is that many physicians don't even know what better care is. The prestigious Institute of Medicine recently published a report that estimates that only about half of what doctors do today is backed up by valid, scientific evidence. The rest? Many procedures and tests are based on medical tradition or on unproven and potentially faulty assumptions about how the body works.

Areas for Change

What all of this suggests is that efforts to rein in our health care costs will have to address the huge number of unnecessary tests, surgeries, doctor visits, and days in the hospital that are all helping to drive up our national medical bill. There are no easy solutions, but let's look at some of the critical areas where a change in practices—and attitudes—is needed.

- *Health information systems.* Though the technology exists to put all of our medical records online, few hospitals or health care systems in the country have invested in it. In most hospitals, paper records not only waste time but also lead to duplication of effort, creating more costly errors. An estimated 20 percent of tests and radiological scans are repeated simply because they can't be located or can't be transmitted from one doctor to another in a timely fashion.

- *Shared decision making.* Doctors say they practice defensive medicine in part to avoid malpractice suits. But a better solution would be reforms that encourage doctors to spend the time needed to explain to patients the trade-offs between potential treatments. Called shared decision making, this kind of interaction could provide more personalized medicine and would also reduce unnecessary care. Evidence suggests that patients who are truly informed about the risks and benefits of a treatment or a test are more satisfied with the choices they make and often less likely to want expensive invasive procedures. One challenge: Physicians would need protection from lawsuits brought by patients who had a bad result from a less aggressive approach.

- *Evidence-based research.* It is essential that we gather better scientific evidence for what works in medicine, what doesn't, and for which patients—and get the word out to doctors. Take the example of spinal fusion to treat acute back pain. We spend more than $16 billion each year on spinal fusions, even though there has never been a rigorous government-funded clinical trial showing that the surgery is superior to other methods of relieving back pain.

- *New ways of paying doctors and hospitals.* To avoid falling into the fee-for-service trap, many of the health care systems that offer the highest quality care have their doctors on salary. Doctors at the Mayo Clinic, for example, all work on salary. This idea is not popular with specialists, the doctors who earn the highest incomes, but many primary care physicians may be willing to try it. Offering decent salaries to primary care doctors would save money by encouraging them to spend the time needed to provide high-quality, low-cost care.

U.S. Health Care Costs Are Excessive Because of Lack of Competition

Ronald Bailey

Ronald Bailey is the science correspondent for Reason *and* Reason.com, *where he writes a weekly science and technology column.*

"Nobody knows anything," is the famous dictum that screenwriter William Goldman once asserted about Hollywood moviemaking. Goldman was saying that movie producers have no clue about whether or not a movie will sell until it hits the theaters. There is no formula for a hit movie.

The Cost of Health Care

Figuring out health care in America is only slightly more complicated and mysterious than making a hit movie. Fifty million Americans are unable to buy health insurance, and premiums have doubled over the past decade. Health care spending in 2009 consumes about $2.5 trillion, more than 17 percent of our gross domestic product. And as spending has skyrocketed, improvements in health outcomes have been real, but modest. What's going on?

On Saturday [October 17, 2009], President Barack Obama denounced two new studies, sponsored by the health insurance industry, which found that current health care reform bills in Congress will increase premium prices for consumers. One study, done for the lobbying group America's Health Insurance Plans by the consultancy PricewaterhouseCoopers, found that the provisions in the Senate bill sponsored by Sen.

Max Baucus (D-Mont.) would add $1,700 a year to the cost of family coverage in 2013 and $600 for a single person. By 2019, family premiums could be $4,000 higher and individual premiums could be $1,500 higher. A weak individual coverage mandate, coupled with a guarantee issue requirement, no pre-existing condition limits, and no rating based on health status would significantly boost insurance premiums.

The Blue Cross [and] Blue Shield Association commissioned a new study by the Oliver Wyman consultancy, which also found that guaranteed issue and community rating mandates coupled with a weak individual mandate would drive up premiums by 50 percent for individual policies and 19 percent for small group plans.

Fifty million Americans are unable to buy health insurance and premiums have doubled over the past decade.

"Every time we get close to passing reform, the insurance companies produce these phony studies as a prescription and say, 'Take one of these, and call us in a decade,'" declared the president. "Well, not this time."

The President's Claims

The president is right that we should always be skeptical of studies that find in favor of the groups that sponsor them. And these two insurance industry–sponsored studies do have their flaws. But the finding that guaranteed issue and community rating mandates increase insurance premium prices has been corroborated by other academic researchers. For example, researchers from MIT [Massachusetts Institute of Technology], the Brookings Institution, and Brigham Young University reported in a 2008 study published in *Forum for Health Economics & Policy* that community rating regulations increased premiums for high-deductible policies for individuals by as much as 17 percent and families by as much 33 percent in the nongroup market. In addition, the researchers found that the "guarantee issue regulations that accompany community rating regulations in New Jersey are associated with premium increases of well over 100 percent for individual and family policies." And as my colleague Peter Suderman recently pointed out, Massachusetts, the one state that combines an individual mandate, community rating, and guaranteed issue, now has the highest premiums for family insurance plans in the country.

President Obama also denounced the insurance industry malefactors for "making this last-ditch effort to stop reform even as costs continue to rise and our health care dollars continue to be poured into their profits, bonuses, and administrative costs that do nothing to make us healthy—that often actually go toward figuring out how to avoid covering people."

Obama is right that administration costs can be quite large. Why would health insurers spend so much money on administration? According to the *New England Journal of Medicine*, the director of the Office of Management and Budget, Peter Orszag, cites evidence that $830 billion is being spent this year on unnecessary care. That represents about 30 percent of all health care spending. Of course, insurers have a big interest in trying to reduce unnecessary spending, so they hire flocks of administrators to negotiate lower rates and to monitor medical spending charged by doctors and hospital administrators. Government health care programs like Medicare don't have to negotiate; government agencies just fix prices, which means they fail to combat waste and fraud effectively.

What about those insurance company profits? Back in July, President Obama asserted that health insurance companies are making "record profits." Not really. The Annenberg Public Policy Center's FactCheck.org reported, "In general, the health insurance industry did poorly toward the end of 2008 and in the first quarter of 2009, so record profits weren't likely in the second quarter." Averaging profits of 3.3 percent, health insurers are the 86th most profitable industry in the U.S., well behind chain restaurants (7.7 percent), electric utilities (6.2 percent), and brewers (18 percent), but ahead of major auto manufacturers (−3.3 percent), resorts and casinos (−8.9 percent), and major airlines (−11 percent).

We'll pass over the president's naked attempt to provoke voter envy about the big paychecks of health insurance executives, since taxing them away entirely would not perceptibly lower the costs of health insurance.

The Monopolistic Market Consolidation

So why have health costs, and especially health insurance premiums, skyrocketed since 2000? Let's look at one plausible theory: market consolidation. In the past two decades, fewer and fewer competitors are exercising more and more monopoly control over health care spending. Case Western Reserve [University] political scientist Joseph White looks at the last time a Democratic administration pushed for health reform. In 1993, recalls White, "costs were expected to quickly hit 14 percent of GDP [gross domestic product] and rise to 18 percent by the end of the decade." But that didn't happen. Why? One plausible story focuses on the rise of health maintenance organizations (HMOs).

The rise of HMOs was enabled by an earlier federal government attempt to rein in health care costs, the Health Maintenance Organization Act of 1973. The idea behind HMOs was that these insurers would control costs by offering a wide array of preventive care to their subscribers. That sounds like a plausible idea until one realizes that people, on average, change insurers every four years or so. An insurer that invested in preventive care was unlikely to reap the cost-saving benefits. Thanks to the spread of HMOs, the 1990s saw the rise in health care expenditures slow down. Why? Chiefly because HMOs fiercely negotiated lower prices from physicians and hospitals. But the era of modest premium price increases didn't last long.

Hospitals and physicians struck back by beginning to consolidate themselves. As hospital mergers produced local monopolies, they were able to increase their prices substantially. "I find that hospitals increase price by roughly 40 percent following the merger of nearby rivals," Leemore Dafny, an economist at the Kellogg School of Management at Northwestern University concluded in a 2008 study. Insurers with relatively few patients could not bargain effectively with the new local health monopolies, and so dropped out of those markets.

According to White, the result of the 1990s' orgy of insurer and provider consolidation was that "there were half as many health plans in 2004 as in 1996." In addition, "in thirty-eight states the largest firm controlled at least one-third of the insurance market; in sixteen states it controlled at least half." In this analysis, insurers and hospitals have evolved into local oligopolies. One plausible story, it seems, is that an ever more monopolistic health care system has been fueling the recent double digit increases in health care costs.

But then you remember, *nobody knows anything* when it comes to health care. In 2003, the Federal Trade Commission issued a report that concluded that there was "no valid empirical basis" for the claim that consolidations among hospitals "have accounted for increases on hospital services." But what about consolidation among insurers? "The insurance industry is congenitally weak in bargaining with supply side of the American health sector," explained Princeton University health economist Uwe Reinhardt on a recent NPR [National Public Radio] Planet Money segment. Reinhardt believes that insurers largely dance to the fiscal tune whistled by hospitals and physicians.

The Absence of the Consumer

Clearly there has been a drastic failure of market competition when it comes to the health care sector. The question is how can market forces of competition be brought to bear on escalating health care costs?

An essential player is absent from the competitive field: the actual consumer of health care services. So long as insurers can extract their premiums from employers and providers can extract payments from insurers, the health care industrial complex has very little incentive to rein in costs.

One plausible story, it seems, is that an ever more monopolistic health care system has been fueling the recent double digit increases in health care costs.

Recent efforts have been made to create so-called consumer-driven health care based on high deductible insurance policies. Because consumers are on the hook for the first several thousand dollars in health care costs, the idea is that savvy consumers will shop around for health care services and thus force insurers and providers to lower their prices. This cost-reducing dynamic works in most other areas of our economy, so why not in health care?

One of the chief problems is that consumers haven't a clue about what their insurance and medical services cost. Hospital chargemasters (essentially comprehensive lists of all charges) typically contain prices for over 20,000 items and services. Sorting through those lists for the best prices would be impossible for consumers. But why should they have to? In markets, the proper dictum is that "nobody has to know everything." Markets are superb at gathering widely dispersed information and resources from millions of people and firms and then distilling that information into prices.

When someone buys a car, they are not confronted with a bill listing separate prices for pistons, radiators, assembly line screw tightening, seats, gas tanks, windows, and so forth. Nor when they buy a hamburger are the prices for the beef, bun, wrapping paper, and special sauce listed and charged for individually. The market has bundled those separate items together into a single price. Competition sparked by consumer demand could unleash a similar simplifying dynamic in which prices for health insurance and medical services become bundled and more transparent.

The Barriers to Competition

So what kind of real reforms could increase health care competition? Congress should aim to break up the system of local monopolies into which our health care sector has devolved. In his Saturday attack on health insurers, President Obama noted that the industry enjoys "a privileged exception from our antitrust laws, a matter that Congress is rightfully reviewing." What he is talking about is the McCarran-Ferguson Act of 1945 that allows state governments to regulate the business of insurance without federal government interference. The act is, in part, responsible for the evolution toward state insurance markets dominated by just a few large insurers. Consumers cannot purchase insurance policies that are not licensed by their state insurance commissions and which do not incorporate all the mandates imposed by those commissions. Congress and the states should open up competition between insurance companies by enabling "regulatory federalism" that would allow individuals and employers to purchase health insurance from other states. As a report from the free-market Cato Institute notes, regulatory federalism would force state insurance commissions to compete among themselves. The result would be that "states that impose unwanted regulatory costs on insurance purchasers would see their residents' business—and their premium tax revenue—go elsewhere."

Barriers to increased competition among health care providers must be removed too. For example, many states have certificate of need programs that forbid the construction of new health care facilities without prior regulatory approval. Passed by Congress in 1974 as a cost-cutting measure, the ostensible purpose of the programs is to keep health care costs low by requiring advance approval by state agencies for most hospital expansions and major equipment purchases. But regulations don't really work that way. "Market incumbents can too easily use [certificate of need] procedures to forestall competitors from entering an incumbent's market," according to a 2004 Federal Trade Commission report. In fact, "programs can actually increase prices by fostering anti-competitive barriers to entry." State-enforced monopolies increase prices? Who knew?

Congress should aim to break up the system of local monopolies into which our health care sector has devolved.

There is one thing that everybody should know when it comes to health care: Competition in markets tends to lower prices and improve quality over time. It can do so in health care markets as well.

CHAPTER 2

Should the Government Help Ensure Access to Health Insurance?

Chapter Preface

O ne of the biggest controversies surrounding the American health care system is the issue of government involvement in ensuring that Americans have access to health care through health insurance. On one end of the debate are those who believe government should completely stay out of the business of health care, allowing the private health insurance market to operate relatively unencumbered. On the other end of the debate are those who believe the government should take complete responsibility for providing health care for all by implementing a government-run, single-payer health care system. In between these two views are a variety of positions on the role of government in health care.

The fact that the American public is divided on the role of government with respect to access to health care is itself unique among nations of the world. According to a 2008 poll by WorldPublicOpinion.org (WPO) of twenty-one nations, the United States was among only a handful of nations—joined by India, the Palestinian territories, Egypt, and Thailand—where less than 90 percent of people believed that government should be responsible for ensuring people can meet their basic need for health care. Only 77 percent of Americans polled thought that government should be responsible.[1] America had the highest percentage among any nation polled—21 percent—of people who affirmatively said that government was not responsible.

A year later, a poll by WPO and the Brookings Institution showed that as the health care debate intensified, the number of people against government responsibility for ensuring access to basic health care had grown significantly. The 2009

1. WorldPublicOpinion.org, "World Publics See Government as Responsible for Ensuring Basic Healthcare, Food, and Education Needs," November 10, 2008.

poll showed that only 60 percent of Americans thought government should be responsible for ensuring people can meet their need for basic health care, while the percentage of people denying such responsibility grew to 37 percent. Views about government responsibility for health care access were split along party lines, with 69 percent of Republicans claiming that government should not be responsible for ensuring access to health care and 86 percent of Democrats claiming that it should.[2]

Among those Americans who believe government should have responsibility for ensuring access to health care, the methodology favored to achieve that end is varied. Only 47 percent of Americans are in favor of the government providing health care services directly. Enacting a mandate that all Americans buy health insurance, requiring employers to offer health insurance, and extending the option of health insurance to all people in America including illegal immigrants are some of the other ways in which government can help ensure access to health care. All are debated in this chapter.

2. Steven Kull, William Galston, and Clay Ramsay, "Battleground or Common Ground? American Public Opinion on Health Care Reform," Brookings Institution and World PublicOpinion.org, October 8, 2009, pp. 7–8. www.brookings.edu.

A Government Mandate
to Buy Health Insurance
Is Constitutional

Timothy Noah

Timothy Noah is a senior writer for Slate *and a contributing writer to the* Washington Monthly.

B arack Obama spent much of the 2008 presidential-primary season arguing with [fellow Democratic candidate] Hillary Clinton about whether health reform should include a so-called "individual mandate" requiring all Americans to purchase health insurance. Clinton argued that it should. Obama argued that it shouldn't (even though his own plan called for a more limited individual mandate requiring parents to purchase health insurance for their children). One of Obama's central arguments was that enforcing such a mandate would be impractical. "You can mandate it," Obama said, "but there still will be people who can't afford it. And if they can't afford it, what are you going to fine them?"

The Insurance Mandate

At the time I thought Obama had the better argument, not just on practicality but also with respect to the Constitution. "If you want to drive a car," I wrote,

> it's accepted that you have to buy private auto insurance. But that's conditional on enjoying the societal privilege of driving a car; you can avoid the requirement by choosing not to drive one. A mandate to buy private health insurance, however, would be conditional on . . . being alive. I can't think of another instance in which the government says out-

right, "You must buy this or that," independent of any special privilege or subsidy it may bestow on you.

Nearly two years later, Obama has made peace with the individual mandate, which is included in the bills that cleared three House committees and one Senate committee. The House bill imposes on anyone who neglects to purchase health insurance for himself or his family a 2.5 percent tax on modified adjusted gross income. The Senate health committee bill imposes a minimum penalty of $750. Yet I've continued to wonder whether the individual mandate is constitutional.

Should health reform pass, it seems a dead certainty that conservatives will go to court to challenge the individual mandate. A preview of their arguments can be found on the Web site of the conservative Federalist Society in the paper, "Constitutional Implications of an 'Individual Mandate' in Health Care Reform" by Peter Urbanowicz, a former deputy general counsel at the Health and Human Services [HHS] department, and Dennis Smith, a former director of HHS's Center for Medicaid and State Operations. One of these turns out to resemble my earlier argument:

> Nearly every state now has a law mandating auto insurance for all drivers. But the primary purpose of the auto insurance mandate was to provide financial protection for people that a driver may harm, and not necessarily for the driver himself. And the auto insurance mandate is a quid pro quo for having the state issuing a privilege: in this case a driver's license.

Should health reform pass, it seems a dead certainty that conservatives will go to court to challenge the individual mandate.

The Commerce Clause

Since I first wrote about this, it's been pointed out to me that the comparison with auto insurance is not a *legal* argument at all. (I am not a lawyer.) The legal question isn't whether it would be unusual for the government to compel people to buy health insurance. It's whether it would square with the Constitution. Mark Hall, a professor of law at Wake Forest University, argues that it would, in part based on the Commerce Clause, which since the New Deal has permitted the federal government to expand its power in various ways by defining various activities as "interstate commerce." Although health *delivery* is often local, Hall writes, "most medical supplies, drugs and equipment are shipped in interstate commerce." More to the point, "most health insurance is sold through interstate companies."

Yes, counter Urbanowicz and Smith, but "it is a different matter to find a basis for imposing Commerce Clause–related regulation on an individual who chooses not to undertake a commercial transaction." Does the Commerce Clause cover your *refusal* to engage in interstate commerce?

The individual mandate requires citizens to fork over not their houses or their automobiles but their money.

Well, yes, Hall in effect answers, because when a person declines to purchase health insurance, that affects interstate commerce, too, by driving up health insurance premiums for everyone else:

> Covering more people is expected to reduce the price of insurance by addressing free-rider and adverse selection problems. Free riding includes relying on emergency care and other services without paying for all the costs, and forcing providers to shift those costs onto people with insurance. Adverse selection is the tendency to wait to purchase until a person expects to need health care, thereby keeping out of the insurance pool a full cross section of both low and higher cost subscribers. Covering more people also could re-

duce premiums by enhancing economies of scale in pooling of risk and managing medical costs.

In essence, the Commerce Clause enables the economic arguments for the individual mandate to become legal arguments as well.

A Taking or a Tax

Urbanowicz and Smith next reach for that perennial conservative favorite, the Fifth Amendment's Takings Clause, which says the government may not take property from a citizen without just compensation. "Requiring a citizen to devote a percent of his or her income for a purpose for which he or she otherwise might not choose based on individual circumstances," Urbanowicz and Smith write, "could be considered an arbitrary and capricious 'taking.' . . ."

But according to Akhil Reed Amar, who teaches constitutional law at Yale, the case law does not support Urbanowicz and Smith. "A taking is paradigmatically singling out an *individual*," Amar explains. The individual mandate (despite its name) applies to everybody. Also, "takings are paradigmatically about real property. They're about *things*." The individual mandate requires citizens to fork over not their houses or their automobiles but their money. Finally, Amar points out, the individual mandate does not result in the state taking something without providing compensation. The health insurance that citizens must purchase *is* compensation. In exchange for paying a premium, the insurer pledges (at least in theory) to pay some or all doctor and hospital bills should the need arise for medical treatment. The individual mandate isn't a *taking*, Amar argues. It's a *tax*.

But how can it be a tax if the money is turned over not to the government but to a private insurance company? William Treanor, dean of Fordham Law School and an expert on takings, repeated much of Amar's analysis to me (like Amar, he thinks a takings-based argument would never get anywhere), but instead of a tax he compared the individual mandate to the federal law mandating a minimum wage. Congress passes a law that says employers need to pay a certain minimum amount not to the government but to any person they hire. "The beneficiaries of that are private actors," Treanor explained. But it's allowed under the Commerce Clause. "Minimum wage law is constitutional." So, too, then, is the individual mandate.

The Government Should Require Employers to Share in Cost of Health Insurance

Families USA

Families USA is a national nonprofit, nonpartisan organization dedicated to the achievement of high-quality, affordable health care for all Americans. A complete list of sources used in this viewpoint is available from Families USA.

Many health reform proposals call for employers, individuals, and the government all to share responsibility for paying for health care. Generally, under these proposals, employers that do not provide coverage for their workers would be required to pay a fee toward the cost of coverage for their employees. Individuals who could afford to obtain coverage would be responsible for doing so, and the government would assist with premiums as needed.

Requiring employers to share the responsibility of paying for health care will create a level playing field among employers of all sizes, and it will help people who are satisfied with their job-based coverage keep that coverage. (About 61 percent of non-elderly Americans get their coverage through an employer.)

There are five reasons why it makes sense to require employers to contribute to the cost of coverage, which is known as an "employer responsibility requirement":

1. Employer assessments help to level the playing field so that all employers do their fair share to pay for coverage.

Families USA, "Why Employers Should Share the Responsibility of Paying for Health Care," *Talking About Health Care Reform*, June 2009, pp. 1–3. Copyright © 2009 Families USA. Reproduced by permission.

2. An employer responsibility requirement will discourage employers from dropping coverage and keep needed dollars in the health care system.
3. Employers that currently pay a share of their employees' health insurance cover a large portion of employees' health bills.
4. Employer assessments have been helpful in places that have implemented them.
5. Job-based health coverage is priced more equitably than individual coverage.

Employer assessments help to level the playing field so that all employers do their fair share to pay for coverage.

Currently, most large employers provide coverage to their workers, but some do not. The most recent government survey showed that nearly 97 percent of employers with 50 or more workers provided coverage to their employees. About 61 percent of employers with fewer than 50 workers provided coverage to their employees.

There are five reasons why it makes sense to require employers to contribute to the cost of coverage.

Whether or not employers provide health coverage is entirely up to them. Even a business that is doing very well financially can decide not to provide health coverage, giving it an advantage over competitors who "do the right thing" by offering coverage to their workers. An assessment system could be designed to level the playing field among businesses of different sizes and financial situations. For example, a system could be created that would exempt the smallest employers or those businesses that could not afford to contribute to employee insurance but that would require businesses to contribute to employee health coverage if they could afford to do so.

Employers that provide coverage end up paying a "hidden health tax" for uncompensated care costs for the uninsured when other employers do not chip in to cover their workers. Premiums are higher because uninsured people who receive health care often cannot afford to pay the full amount themselves, and the costs of their care are shifted to those who have insurance.

An employer responsibility requirement will discourage employers from dropping coverage and keep needed dollars in the health care system.

Because health reform is likely to make individual coverage more accessible, without an employer responsibility requirement, employers may be tempted to drop the coverage that they now provide to their employees. In addition, the money that employers pay for worker coverage represents a significant chunk of the overall funding of the health care system. In 2006, altogether, employers paid health insurance premiums totaling nearly $360 billion, and that amount has continued to rise over the years. If employers drop employee coverage, the share of overall health care costs that they currently pay could not easily be replaced.

If employers dropped employee coverage and employees had to find coverage in the individual market, they could be forced to pay higher premiums.

Employers that currently pay a share of their employees' health insurance cover a large portion of employees' health bills.

In 2008, employers paid an average of $9,325 for family coverage, and employees paid $3,354. For coverage of single individuals, employers paid an average of $3,983, and employees paid $721. If employers were to stop contributing to the cost of coverage, most employees would not be able to fill the gap by themselves. Either the federal government would have to step in and subsidize that coverage, or employees would be left with unaffordable costs.

Employer assessments have been helpful in places that have implemented them.

In Massachusetts, employers that do not contribute their "fair share" (as determined by state rules) to their workers' health care pay a $295 annual assessment. Even though the state now subsidizes individual coverage, there has been no evidence that making individual coverage more affordable has encouraged employers to drop coverage. In fact, between June 2006 and March 2008, 159,000 Massachusetts residents gained job-based coverage.

Under a San Francisco ordinance, employers with 20–99 workers must spend at least $1.23/hour on each worker's health care, and employers with 100 or more workers must spend at least $1.85/hour on each worker's health care. Employers can show that they are meeting this obligation by directly paying for health services, providing health insurance, funding health savings accounts (HSAs) or medical reimbursement accounts that employees can use to cover out-of-pocket medical expenses, or paying into a new city-funded program called "Healthy San Francisco" to provide health care for their employees. By January 2009, 32,804 employees whose employers did not otherwise contribute to their health care received some help by virtue of the new obligation.

Job-based health coverage is priced more equitably than individual coverage.

For example, all similar workers within a firm pay the same premiums, regardless of their age or health status. This is not the case in the individual health insurance market, where insurance companies can vary premiums based on age, health status, and a host of other factors. If employers dropped employee coverage and employees had to find coverage in the individual market, they could be forced to pay higher premiums based on their age or other characteristics.

The Government Should Help Illegal Immigrants Get Health Insurance

Andrew Romano

Andrew Romano is a senior writer for Newsweek, *who reports on politics, culture, and food.*

Call it the shout heard round the world. Since last Wednesday [September 9, 2009] when Rep. Joe Wilson, Republican of South Carolina, interrupted [President] Barack Obama's big speech on health care reform to shout "You lie!" Beltway bloviators have bloviated about little else. Wilson's vulgarity. Wilson's apology. Wilson's "dirty health care secret." Wilson's charming effort to make American politics more British.

And that's just at *Newsweek*.

Health Insurance for Illegal Immigrants

Few of us, however, have actually bothered to address the issue that provoked Wilson's outburst: health insurance for illegal immigrants. The line he objected to—"The reforms I'm proposing would not apply to those who are here illegally"—is, in fact, not a "lie." The current House bill makes it very clear that "individuals who are not lawfully present in the United States" will not be allowed to receive subsidies. To wrangle assistance, illegal aliens would have to commit identity fraud, something that rarely happens in our current public health care system (a.k.a. Medicare). And Democratic senators have just announced that they'll require those who participate to show proof of citizenship. So it's a non-issue.

But let's just assume, for argument's sake, that we all live in Wilsonville, where Obama is the lying liar his critics allege him to be—the sort of psycho who has chosen to sacrifice his political future on the flaming pyre of anti-immigrant sentiment by concocting a secret scheme to cover the nation's estimated 11.9 million illegals. Would that really be so bad?

From a purely economic standpoint, insuring illegal immigrants makes a lot of sense—and not just for them, but for everyone.

Of course, insuring undocumented workers is ethically murky and politically impossible. Some people argue that if we're hiring illegals to, say, shingle our roofs, we have a moral obligation to care for them if they fall off. But more people, it seems, simply want them out of the country. Given that illegal immigrants have, by definition, broken our laws, it makes sense that large numbers of upstanding citizens oppose any measure that would encourage more foreigners to sneak into America or make their lives easier once they're here.

The Economic Benefits

The only problem? From a purely economic standpoint, insuring illegal immigrants makes a lot of sense—and not just for them, but for everyone.

Consider a few statistics. According to a July article in the *American Journal of Public Health*, immigrants typically arrive in America during their prime working years and tend to be younger and healthier than the rest of the U.S. population. As a result, health care expenditures for the average immigrant are 55 percent lower than for a native-born American citizen with similar characteristics. With the ratio of seniors to workers projected to increase by 67 percent between 2010 and 2030, it stands to reason that including the relatively healthy, relatively employable and largely uninsured illegal population in some sort of universal health care system would be a boon rather than a burden. "Insurance in principle has to cover the average medical cost of all the people it's serving," explains Leighton Ku, a professor of health policy at George Washington University. "So if you add cheaper people to the pool, like immigrants, you reduce the average cost." More undocumented workers, in other words, means lower premiums for everyone.

Despite the potential economic upside, the Right shouldn't stress: America won't insure its illegal immigrants any time soon.

The actuarial advantages don't end there. As it is now, undocumented workers (and others) who can't pay their way receive free emergency and charitable care—a service that costs those of us with health insurance an additional $1,000 per year, as Obama noted. But if illegals were covered, this hidden tax would decrease, further lowering our premiums and "relieving some of the financial burden on state and local governments," says Harold Pollack, a University of Chicago professor who specializes in poverty and public health. What's more, employers currently have a clear economic incentive to hire undocumented immigrants: They don't require coverage. A plan that mandates insurance for native workers but not their illegal counterparts actually makes life harder on the blue-collar Americans competing for jobs (and railing against immigrants) because it means that hiring them will cost more than hiring a recent transplant from Mexico City. As the *Washington Post*'s Ezra Klein recently explained, "If you're really worried about the native-born workforce, what you want to do is minimize the differences in labor costs between different types of workers. A health care policy that enlarges those differences—that makes documented workers more expensive compared to undocumented workers—is actually worse for the documented workers."

Money and Politics

At this point, you're probably wondering whether taxpayers would have to foot a bigger bill for these newly insured illegals. Not necessarily—at least in theory. As Obama said in Wednesday's speech, "Like any private insurance company, the public insurance option would have to be self-sufficient and rely on the premiums it collects" to fund whatever care it provides. Given that many undocumented workers leave the country before they're old enough to require much medical care, says Phillip Longman of the New America Foundation, "you could set up the system in a way that they wind up contributing as much or more than they receive" in low-income subsidies, especially when the "offsetting savings of lower emergency room use" are factored in.

But despite the potential economic upside, the Right shouldn't stress: America won't insure its illegal immigrants any time soon. "The hard thing here is that the current state of perception on immigration is eroding our sense of social solidarity," says Longman, who believes, like the rest of the experts quoted in this story, that covering undocumented workers is both politically and logistically impractical. "People simply don't want money going to people on the other side of the tracks." That pretty much explains why Obama was so determined to clear up the confusion—and why Joe Wilson was so determined to keep it alive. Never mind that our wallets would be better off if Wilson were right. Money, after all, isn't everything—even in politics.

A Government Mandate to Buy Health Insurance Is a Violation of Liberty

Robert Moffit

Robert Moffit is director of the Heritage Foundation's Center for Health Policy Studies and a former senior official at the U.S. Department of Health and Human Services.

In his address to Congress, President [Barack] Obama made clear that he and his allies know how to spend your health care money better than you do. It's a matter, you see, of "shared responsibility": You share your dollars with the feds, and the feds are responsible for making your decisions. In the health care bill currently [October 2009] before the House (H.R. 3200), there is even a "Health Choices Commissioner," to be appointed by the president, who will rigorously define your choices.

The Individual Mandate

On "shared responsibility," the president brooks no dissent. "Unless everybody does their part, many of the insurance reforms we seek—especially requiring insurance companies to cover preexisting conditions—just can't be achieved," he said. "That's why under my plan, individuals will be required to carry basic health insurance." This requirement is known as the "individual mandate."

The president's proposal is historic—though not in a good way. Never before has Congress forced Americans to buy a private good or service. In fact, for those with a traditional understanding of the Constitution as a charter of liberty (as

Robert Moffit, "At What Cost to Freedom?" *National Review Online*, October 5, 2009. Copyright © 2009 by National Review, Inc., 215 Lexington Avenue, New York, NY 10016. Reproduced by permission.

opposed to the "living" version), the list of Congress's powers in Article I, Section 8, grants it no authority to require any such thing.

The Obama administration, along with its allies in Congress and throughout health policy wonkdom, would have you believe that, on the question of a mandate, everyone of sound reputation is in agreement. That's not true; there is no consensus on this issue, any more than there is a consensus on the "public option."

Penalties for Noncompliance

For one thing, mandates are meaningless without penalties for noncompliance, and polling data suggests that Americans might accept an individual mandate, but not the penalties. This became a problem for Hillary Clinton in the 2008 presidential primaries, when Obama strongly disagreed with her proposal to impose an individual mandate—saying, among other things, that it was unenforceable (he cited noncompliance with auto insurance laws as evidence). Clinton responded by suggesting such measures as tax penalties and wage garnishments for health insurance scofflaws, which Obama knew would be unpopular with voters.

The president's proposal is historic—though not in a good way.

Now that Obama is president, he no longer objects to such penalties. In the House bill, everyone would be required to have an "acceptable" health plan (as defined by law) or pay a penalty of 2.5 percent of his adjusted gross income. This penalty is expected to bring in $29 billion over a ten-year period. In the Senate Health, Education, Labor, & Pensions Committee bill, the penalty is set at 50 percent of the price of the lowest-cost health plan participating in the bill's state-run health insurance exchanges. That's expected to generate $36 billion over ten years.

Meanwhile, Sen. Max Baucus (D., Mont.) has unveiled a Senate Finance Committee draft that also has an individual mandate. It would levy a penalty of up to $3,800 on families for what the president calls "irresponsible behavior," by which he means health care choices of which he disapproves. In Obama's usage, "personal responsibility" is selective; it doesn't extend to the question of taking responsibility for one's health care. That's the government's job. Of course, federal officials will have outside help in deciding for the rest of us. Powerful special interest groups and health industry lobbyists will do all they can to make sure that their favored medical treatments, procedures, drugs, and devices are part of the "bare minimum" that every plan must include.

A Hidden Tax

Despite all this, the president is right on one key point: The current system makes those with health coverage pay for those without. And those who are without health coverage often get their care in the most expensive place possible: the hospital emergency room. The president correctly calls this a hidden tax. Under existing federal law, hospitals are required to provide treatment to everyone who comes to their emergency room, regardless of his ability to pay. There is no serious legislation under consideration that would change that.

About three-quarters of this uncompensated care, adding up to tens of billions of dollars annually, is financed, in some way, by the taxpayers. (Health care providers absorb some of these costs by delivering charity care.) The extent and degree of this cost shifting varies from state to state. The challenge for conservatives is to address the situation in a practical way that does not reward personal irresponsibility—the free-rider problem—or curtail freedom. That means taking the principle of "personal responsibility" seriously by making sure that personal choices are clearly defined and consequential.

The Mandate in Massachusetts

The experience of Massachusetts shows how hard it can be to pull off this balancing act. In 2005, as the state faced $1.3 billion per year in taxpayer-financed uncompensated health care costs, Republican governor Mitt Romney came up with a plan. In sum, his position was that people should exercise their responsibility by choosing their own health insurance and paying their own health care bills. The state would provide direct assistance to help low-income folks buy insurance, drawing heavily from existing government funding of health care.

Under the Romney proposal, those who did not wish to buy health insurance would be allowed to self-insure, but they would have to post a $10,000 bond to pay their health care bills, such as hospital emergency care, instead of shifting them onto the taxpayer. Anyone who refused to do so would lose an exemption on his state income tax.

Requiring everyone to buy government-specified health insurance, whether they need it or not, is an unacceptable violation of personal liberty.

Romney's proposal, strictly speaking, was not a requirement to purchase health insurance; it was a requirement to pay one's health bills, through insurance or predetermined direct payment, thus reducing the burden on taxpayers. Nonetheless, it satisfied nobody. Critics on the Right, especially libertarians, said it amounted to a health insurance mandate, while those on the Left said it was a weak and unnecessary substitute for the "real thing," which the Massachusetts legislature enacted in 2006: a straight mandate for individuals to buy health insurance or pay a fine.

That mandate fell short of universal coverage. Some 60,000 people, roughly 1 percent of the state's population, were initially exempted, as state officials—fearing a political backlash from labor officials, among others—refrained from imposing the mandate on some low-income people they believed would have trouble paying for insurance. So, while the state's liberal legislature allowed the government to set generous required benefit levels, politicians continued to steer money to favored hospitals, aggravating the state's health care cost crisis. In other words, they deliberately weakened a key element of Romney's proposed reform, which was to redirect existing government funding from institutions to individuals and families. The Massachusetts experiment reminds us that in health care policy, precision in drafting and careful implementation count as much as the broad outlines of legislation.

Freedom and Responsibility

In Massachusetts or Washington, no individual mandate is going to achieve the goal of universal coverage. In the cases of similar mandates—auto insurance, income tax filing, military draft registration—compliance has invariably fallen short of universal. The better course of action is to be serious about both personal freedom and personal responsibility. They go together; you cannot have one without the other. And under the House and Senate bills, we would have neither.

Requiring everyone to buy government-specified health insurance, whether they need it or not, is an unacceptable violation of personal liberty. It is a way of taxing healthy people without calling it a tax. Since that is an irresistible temptation to politicians, the list of required benefits would be certain to keep expanding.

The choice between freedom and responsibility, as the president and his congressional allies portray it, is a false choice. We can and should have both.

The Government Should Not Require Employers to Provide Health Insurance

James M. Thunder

James M. Thunder is a lawyer in Washington, D.C.

On June 15 [2009], before the American Medical Association meeting in Chicago, President [Barack] Obama proclaimed: "While I believe every business has a responsibility to provide health insurance for its workers, small businesses that can't afford it should receive an exemption." He had made a similar statement in a June 2 letter to Senators [Edward M.] Kennedy and [Max] Baucus, chairmen of two Senate committees drafting health care legislation. He wrote that he was open to proposals that would "ask . . . employers [to] share in the cost" while "small businesses . . . should be exempted." In neither instance did he use the term "employer mandate," but small business could not be "exempt" from anything other than an otherwise applicable mandate.

An Employer Mandate

An "employer mandate"—by which employers must pay for the health care (that is, health insurance) of their employees or pay a tax—assumes that an employer has an obligation to care for the health of his or her employees. Upon what does such an expectation rest? To use a term President Obama would understand from his days teaching constitutional law, what is the "rational relationship" between being an employer and paying for the health care of an employee?

Let's cut to the chase. There is *no* rational relationship. Of course, an employer is obliged to provide a workplace that is

James M. Thunder, "The Employer Mandate and the Alternative," *American Spectator*, June 22, 2009. Copyright © The American Spectator 2009. Reproduced by permission.

safe, that is conducive to the employees' health. The "employer mandate" as being used in the current debate on health care legislation is not restricted, however, to providing a safe workplace but extends to the health generally of the employee. Furthermore, it is not restricted to employees, but also to their spouses and children.

The expectation, the relationship, rests on history. Employers started giving health insurance to their employees and dependents during World War II in an effort by employers to compete in the marketplace for employees when the government would not allow them to compete for employees based on wages (since there were wage and price controls). The federal government agreed not to count this as income to employees. After wage and price controls were lifted, employers continued—to this day—to compete for employees by offering health insurance. By now, the Kaiser Family Foundation reports, two-thirds of Americans under age 65 (158 million) have health care coverage through their employer.

An "employer mandate" . . . assumes that an employer has an obligation to care for the health of his or her employees.

The Downward Trend in Employer Coverage

Health insurance premiums have become ever larger. This is reflected in the taxes that would otherwise have been received by the U.S. Treasury from individuals—$240 billion per year. (As [patient advocate] Betsy McCaughey points out [in the July–August 2009 *American Spectator*], however, the American people devote about the same share of their income for food, energy, housing and health care now as they did in 1960.)

For the past decade, as health insurance premiums have increased, there has been a downward trend in the scope of employer coverage. Instead of more and more employers offering better and better coverage, employers are decreasing their contributory share to the health insurance of their employees (thereby raising the share of the employees' contribution) and many have stopped offering health insurance as a benefit of employment. Without insurance, the employee is often (not always) left with buying individual policies without the cost advantage of belonging to a group. (President Obama, like so many others, refers to the number of uninsured as 46 million, a figure that includes, as Betsy McCaughey noted, the 14 million who are eligible for public aid and the 24 million who have sufficient funds to purchase insurance but choose not to do so.)

Employer Benefits

Asserting that health care is essential to every person, asserting that health insurance is important to every person, does not logically lead us to the assertion that employers must be required by law to pay for the health insurance of their employees and their dependents. By this reasoning, we could just as well assert that, since food, clothing, shelter and education are also essential, government should mandate employers to provide these.

The rapacious Democrats will require employers to provide health care to employees because employers are regarded as having the money.

Indeed, there are some employers who provide employees and their dependents with food, clothing (a uniform), shelter (company-owned and gated) and education (private schooling for minors). And 24/7 security. And transportation once or twice yearly to visit relatives. And rotational cycles of 30 days on, 30 days off. And a car allowance. And life and disability and vision and dental insurance. And a defined pension. And stock options. And a high salary. No, these perks are not limited to top management. In yesteryear some of these perks were granted to residents of company towns, such as the Pullman neighborhood of Chicago, and Hershey, Pennsylvania. Today, employers routinely give these benefits to "expats" (expatriates), that is, employees who work in countries other than their home countries.

Under what circumstances will our government mandate employers to provide the same perks expats receive to *all* of their employees regardless of where they work? It would seem there are two criteria: if the benefit is deemed essential and if the benefit costs a lot of money.

I think the rapacious Democrats are like Willie Sutton. When asked why he robbed banks, he reputedly answered, "Because that's where the money is." The rapacious Democrats will require employers to provide health care to employees because employers are regarded as having the money.

Jobs run the gamut from those with low pay, hard work, and no benefits to "good jobs" consisting of high pay, light work, and a plenitude of benefits. People aspire to obtain "a good job." If the government should intervene in the market and mandate that every employer provide health insurance to every employee (and their dependents), then all jobs will have health insurance, thereby restricting the ability of employers to compete for employees and reducing the incentive of people to compete for jobs.

You may respond that an employer mandate for health insurance is similar to the mandate of a 40-hour work week or an 8-hour day or maternity leave. But health insurance is not like these other mandates. These other mandates are related directly to work and the workplace. An employer mandate for health insurance is more like the government mandating employers to provide affordable housing to every employee or mandating a defined pension or a minimum contribution to employees' 401(k) accounts.

The Size of Business

Oh, the president will consider exempting small business. Tell me, how will the government define "a small business"? Will the criteria change over time so that what is deemed small today will be deemed big tomorrow? (This was Joe "the Plumber" Wurzelbacher's critique during the 2008 presidential campaign, on CBS News, Oct. 15.) Why would a small business want to grow into a big business if, after it meets an IRS [Internal Revenue Service] threshold, it will be required to provide health insurance for all of its employees? And why would an individual start a business knowing that, if he or she is successful, he or she will be required to pay for health insurance for every employee—not because the market requires it to attract employees but because the government requires it?

Once we distinguish in principle between businesses that would be subject to a mandate and those that would not be, it allows us to consider distinctions other than big/small. What about businesses that create health hazards and those that do not? Let's focus on the president's language in his June 2 letter concerning "unmanaged chronic diseases" or the reference in his June 25 speech to "[f]ive of the costliest illnesses and conditions—cancer, cardiovascular disease, diabetes, lung disease, and strokes." President Obama cited Safeway in his June 15 speech. As Steven A. Burd, the CEO of Safeway, reported in the June 12 issue of the *Wall Street Journal*, that company, a self-insured employer, has reduced employee contributions to health insurance for particular employees, as allowed by HIPAA (1996 Health Insurance Portability and Accountability Act) if the employee can show improvement in the following areas: tobacco usage, weight, blood pressure and cholesterol levels. Thus, instead of distinguishing between big and small businesses, the government could mandate that companies that exacerbate these, and other, health problems pay for the health insurance of *all* of us. Among these would be junk food makers, tobacco companies, TV and video entertainment (think couch potato, with an exemption for Wii), manufacturers and dealers of less-safe cars, and gun manufacturers and dealers.

The Role of Government

Permit me to make another couple of points about the Democrats' plans. First, the government will necessarily have to dictate the minimum elements of the health insurance mandated of employers: maximum deductibles, maximum co-pays, drug coverage, minimum lifetime limits, abortion coverage, same-sex spouse coverage, polygamous spouse coverage, *in vitro* fertilization for unwed employees, and on and on.

Second, the president's letter (and later his speech) included the following argument for establishing a government-run insurance program to which every American could subscribe (commonly called "the public option"): "I strongly believe that Americans should have the choice of a public health insurance option operating alongside private plans. This will give them a better range of choices, make the health care market more competitive, and keep insurance companies honest." By the same reasoning, the government could establish a government-owned car manufacturer (indeed it has), a government-owned bank (indeed it has), a government-owned television station, a government-owned chain of pizza parlors—all to make the market more competitive and keep the private sector competitors honest.

Changes Consistent with American Liberties

My response is this: Any health care legislation enacted by a legislature established by the United States Constitution should enhance our freedoms—the freedoms of employers, of employees, of health care providers, of health insurance carriers. We must find a way for our government to encourage entities *other than employers* to offer health insurance and offer them the opportunity to do so *across state boundaries.* This would provide an exponential increase in competition, freedom of choice for all, and no worries by individuals about portability from job to job or about preexisting conditions.

Imagine this if you would: You belong to an association devoted to the cure of juvenile diabetes. Under new legislation, the association offers health insurance to all of its members—with the profits from its health insurance program going to fund research for the cure.

Americans belong to a host of associations and organizations: fraternal organizations like the Elks, Optimists, Shriners, Knights of Columbus; churches, synagogues and mosques; unions; ethnic groups such as NAACP [National Association for the Advancement of Colored People], Ancient Order of Hibernians, [National Council of] La Raza; Daughters of the American Revolution; college alumni associations; National Rifle Association—you name it. Each of these could be incentivized to provide one or more plans of health insurance to members. These entities could bargain on behalf of thousands of members for group rates, or even self-insure. You could select a plan to meet the needs of you and your family from one of the entities to which you belong. You would not be dependent on your employer for health insurance.

Any health care legislation enacted by a legislature established by the United States Constitution should enhance our freedoms.

Just as the law has incentivized employers since World War II to provide health insurance for employees, the law could incentivize non-employers to do so. Although an employer could continue to provide health insurance, nearly every employer would see that it would be better to give a voucher to employees who could choose their own plan from various sources. At the same time, the employer could eliminate from its budget the administrative burden of negotiating with an insurance provider and administering the insurance plan.

We are constantly told that now—this summer—is the time to reform the health care system in America. If we are to enact changes, let us resolve to make changes consistent with American liberties. Having the government mandate that employers provide health insurance, having the government create distinctions between big and small businesses, having the government establish minimum health care coverage, and having the government incorporate a government-owned health insurance carrier does not qualify as change consistent with American liberties.

The Government Should Not Help Illegal Immigrants Get Health Insurance

James R. Edwards Jr.

James R. Edwards Jr. is a fellow at the Center for Immigration Studies, an independent, nonpartisan, nonprofit research organization.

A *Washington Post* editorial Saturday [December 26, 2009] argues that illegal aliens should be allowed to purchase health insurance through the "exchange" created in both the House and Senate health reform bills. The argument is a familiar one in health policy circles. Having more people in the insurance pool means rendering less uncompensated care that burdens hospitals and other providers. The *Post* adds that illegal aliens tend to be younger and thus should amount to a net gain to the insurance risk pool; they'd pay premiums while seeking medical services relatively less often.

The House bill allows illegal immigrants access to the exchange, while the Senate bill excludes them. And the House applies the individual mandate, requiring most people to have health insurance, to illegal aliens, while the Senate bill exempts illegals from the mandate.

Illegal Immigrants and Health Insurance

The editors of Washington's liberal newspaper assume a lot. They assume illegal aliens want health insurance. The rates of uninsurance among illegal immigrants to date, compared with their remittances sent to relatives back home, indicate that obtaining health coverage may not be a high priority for a lot of illegal aliens. Many could (and do) find some form of afford-

James R. Edwards Jr., "*Washington Post*'s Take on Illegals in Health Reform," Center for Immigration Studies, December 27, 2009. Reproduced by permission.

able health insurance today if they were willing to buy it. But many would apparently rather spend their money on other things, including remittances of amounts about equal to the premiums of low-cost insurance policies or health savings accounts.

The *Post* assumes illegals don't have access to medical care without insurance. However, many receive medical services from "safety net" providers whenever they wish. The federal EMTALA [Emergency Medical Treatment and Active Labor Act] law guarantees that anyone without insurance can demand "emergency" medical care, regardless of immigration status, insurance status, or ability to pay. And that can have dire consequences for everyone else in a community—such as bankrupting hospitals in Southern California and Arizona, and causing cost shifting that increases the health care costs of responsible people who are insured. . . .

Congress considered an amendment in 1996 to immigration reform that would have tied federal payment for illegals' uncompensated medical care to having the recipient hospitals and clinics to supply information on those illegal aliens to immigration authorities. The amendment was rejected when medical special interests weighed in that they wanted their candy without the spinach.

The rates of uninsurance among illegal immigrants to date . . . indicate that obtaining health coverage may not be a high priority for a lot of illegal aliens.

It's true the uninsured may not benefit from some preventive services or regular checkups. But pretty much every medical screening and routine service is available to anyone, including illegal aliens, at no or nominal cost almost anywhere in America. Often, such services come from a private-sector medical provider. Seeking out such medical attention rests with the person who needs it and, again, this seems a lower priority to illegal aliens.

An Economic Burden

The *Post* also assumes that insuring illegal immigrants will amount to a net gain. It assumes these people will pay for insurance without the taxpayer subsidy created by the health reform bills. It assumes they will pay more without using more services. But research generally shows that medical care utilization rates rise as people gain health coverage. It's highly likely that newly insured illegal aliens will go to the doctor or clinic more often after they get coverage. . . .

Such "free" health care would increase even more the incentive to immigrate outside the law.

In fact, a major concern in health care circles is whether the health system can accommodate all the newly insured and the services they're sure to demand. And anyone the least bit familiar with economics should warn the *Post* and Congress that increased demand and relatively reduced supply causes costs to go up, not down. That sets up the specter of the government, under the health "reform" regime, playing God: rationing care, choosing winners and losers, putting cost considerations above all else.

Post editors aren't much concerned whether illegal aliens receive taxpayer-funded subsidies in the exchange to pay their insurance premiums. Yet that subsidy, which the Senate makes some attempt to prevent from going to illegals, unjustly would force lawfully resident Americans to pay their own plus foreign lawbreakers' health premiums. Paying tax money for illegal aliens' emergency care already happens and remains unchanged in the legislation. That's bad enough. But forcing extra payment on the backs of people living here lawfully would unduly make illegal residents better off than they already are and in many cases better off than their American counterparts. It's effectively a reward for breaking immigration laws. It's unjust, unfair, and partial. And such "free" health care would increase even more the incentive to immigrate outside the law.

CHAPTER 3

Would a Public Health Insurance Option Be Beneficial?

Overview: American Public Opinion on a Public Option

Steven Kull, William Galston, and Clay Ramsay

Steven Kull is the director of WorldPublicOpinion.org and the Program on International Policy Attitudes (PIPA). William Galston is a former policy advisor to President Bill Clinton and a senior fellow at the Brookings Institution. Clay Ramsay is co-founder and director of research at PIPA.

A majority favors a public option available to all, while three-quarters favor one limited to those who cannot get insurance through their employers. Interestingly, a modest majority of Republicans, as well as large majorities of Democrats and Independents, favors a limited public option.

Arguments for and Against a Public Option

To offer respondents an opportunity to think through the types of arguments frequently repeated in the health care debate, respondents evaluated an argument in favor of each specific proposal and one against it, and only then said whether they favored or opposed the proposal.

The public option was introduced in the following language. The question was preceded by one that described government health care, in part to ensure that respondents would make the clear distinction between it and the public option.

One option is not to have the government provide health services directly but to provide health insurance. The US government currently provides health insurance to senior citizens through Medicare. Some people have proposed giving other

Steven Kull, William Galston, and Clay Ramsay, "Battleground or Common Ground? American Public Opinion on Health Care Reform," Washington, DC: Governance Studies at The Brookings Institution and WorldPublicOpinion.org, 2009. Copyright © 2009 The Brookings Institution. Reproduced by permission.

Americans the option of getting insurance from the government, in addition to the option of private insurance. This is known as providing a "public option."

Respondents then evaluated a dual argument in favor of the public option that mentioned both the uninsured and the benefits of competition:

> If people cannot find affordable coverage the government needs to provide them with an option. Furthermore, the competition provided by a public option would force private insurers to lower their overhead costs, making insurance cheaper for everyone.

This argument was found convincing by 68% and unconvincing by 31%. Slightly more found it very convincing (23%) than found it very unconvincing (15%).

Next an opposing argument was offered that described the competition as inherently unfair and raised the prospect of an eventual complete government takeover of health care:

> Because the government would not need to make profits, a government-run health insurance program would unfairly undercut private insurance companies. This would inevitably lead to a government takeover of health care and put the government between you and your doctor.

Fifty-two percent said they found the argument convincing (20% very), while 46% said it was unconvincing (16% very).

Thus, both the pro and con arguments were found convincing by a majority, though a far larger majority found the pro argument convincing. A substantial number—32%—found both arguments convincing.

A Generally Available Public Option

Finally, respondents were asked whether they favored or opposed "creating a government-administered health insurance option that anyone can purchase to compete with private insurance plans." A 57% majority favored a generally available public option, with 39% opposed.

Overall it appears that hearing the pro and con arguments had little net effect. This exact question was asked by Research 2000 over September 28–30 [2009] and found 59% in support, with 34% opposed.

Among the 32% who found both the pro and the con arguments convincing, asked to decide, 60% came down in favor of a widely available public option, with only 35% opposed.

A Limited Public Option

In the current debate at the level of Congress and the White House, discussion about the public option largely revolves around the goal of providing it to those who are unable to obtain health insurance through an employer. Therefore, in the study, respondents who opposed the widely available public option were then asked, "What if the government-administered health insurance plan were offered as an option only to people who cannot get insurance through their employers?"

> Both the pro and con arguments were found convincing by a majority, though a far larger majority found the pro argument convincing.

Another 18% of the full sample supported this narrower version of the public option. Thus overall, 75% would support a public option as a choice for those who cannot get employer-based health insurance.

Partisan Differences

As would be predicted, Republicans show less support for the public option than Democrats, but interestingly, a majority of Republicans (59%) favors a limited public option, though a large majority (65%) opposes a widely available public option. A substantial majority of Independents favors a generally available option (57%) and a large majority a limited public option (74%). Democrats favor both versions by overwhelming majorities (79% general, 91% limited).

The argument in favor of the public option was found convincing by 52% of Republicans (48% unconvincing), as well as 61% of Independents (39% unconvincing), and 87% of Democrats. The argument opposing the public option was convincing to 70% of Republicans, but unconvincing to 58% of Independents (40% convincing), and 56% of Democrats.

Polling from Other Sources

Recent polling on the public option from other organizations has produced a range of responses, from a divided response to two-thirds in favor. Response was divided over an NBC/*Wall Street Journal* (Sept 17–20 [2009]) question that asked about "creating a public health care plan administered by the government that would compete directly with private health insurance companies." This question did not clarify that the public option would be insurance, as opposed to government-provided health care. It also did not clarify that the purpose was to expand coverage, stating only that it would compete with private companies. When the same question was asked in the context of a list of other options that referred to expanding coverage, support was higher at 53%, perhaps because the potential for greater coverage was implied.

Republicans show less support for the public option than Democrats.

A Kaiser [Family Foundation] poll described the public option as a "government-administered public health *insurance* option" in the context of other options and found 59% in support (September 11–18 [2009]).

CBS/*New York Times* (Sept. 19–23 [2009]) asked about "offering everyone a government-administered health insurance plan—something like the Medicare coverage that people 65 and older get" and found 65% in support. In this case, the description emphasized that it was an insurance plan and made elaborate comparisons to Medicare coverage, which emphasized its purpose of increasing coverage.

A Public Plan Option Is Necessary for Competition

John Holahan and Linda J. Blumberg

John Holahan is director of the Health Policy Research Center, and Linda J. Blumberg is an economist and senior fellow at the Urban Institute, a nonpartisan research organization.

Unfortunately, the debate over whether to provide a public health insurance option as a competitor to private plans under comprehensive health care reform seems to have become an ideological litmus test. Conservatives are fervently aligned against the option while liberals are as strongly in favor of it. Those who oppose it fear that the public plan will have so many inherent advantages that private plans will be unable to compete, eventually leaving the system entirely in government hands by destroying a competitive insurance market. Supporters believe that a public plan is a critical fallback option in a universal system that would cover many high-need and low-income groups.

The arguments around the public plan too often ignore what we believe is the central reason for including a public plan as a component of reform: that health insurance markets today, by and large, are simply not competitive. And as such, these markets are not providing the benefits one would expect from competition, including efficient operations and consequent control over health care costs. We believe that the concentration in the insurance and hospital industries that has taken place over the past several years has been a significant contributor to this problem. The role of the government plan is to counter the adverse impacts of market concentration and, in doing so, slow the growth in health care costs. . . .

Competition in Insurance and Hospital Markets

Economic theory offers a clear description of the characteristics of competitive markets. These include the following:

- Many buyers and sellers participate in the market for a particular good.

- Buyers must be able to make comparisons on price and characteristics of the goods that are offered by the various sellers. Sellers should be able to freely enter or exit the market.

- Economic profits are driven to zero in equilibrium (i.e., all income is devoted to paying for the inputs used in the process of production).

- Each buyer and seller takes the market price as the outcome of competition; in other words, they cannot determine prices.

Health insurance markets very often lack these characteristics. First, in recent years, there has been a great deal of consolidation among health insurers. [James C.] Robinson found that in 36 of the 50 states, three or fewer insurers accounted for 65 percent of the commercial market in 2003. Thirty-four states had values of the Herfindahl-Hirschman Index (a measure of market concentration) that exceeded federal guidelines that deem industries of anti-trust concern. According to a 2008 analysis in 42 states and 314 metropolitan statistical areas (MSAs) done for the American Medical Association, consolidation among insurers continues. Ninety-four percent of the MSAs studied were highly concentrated according to Department of Justice/Federal Trade Commission standards. In 89 percent of MSAs, one health insurer had at least 30 percent of the commercial health insurance market, while one insurer had at least 50 percent of the insurance market in 15 entire states.

Second, there is considerable variation in health insurance products sold, and consumers have great difficulty in making price and quality comparisons. This is especially true in the private non-group insurance market, but is increasingly true in commercial group insurance as well. Covered services and cost-sharing requirements vary not only across insurance firms but across products sold within a single firm. In most non-group insurance markets, the products a firm is willing to sell will even vary with the characteristics of the purchaser, with those with current or past health issues often offered plans with fewer covered benefits. Plans may vary considerably in provider networks as well. While reform would ideally prohibit insurers from offering less comprehensive products to individuals with worse health status, how much uniformity in benefit packages and cost-sharing will be required is unclear, and provider networks will certainly continue to vary across plans. Where there is variation, such as benefit limits and which services count toward out-of-pocket maximums, consumers may not understand the implications until they become ill. As a consequence, making comparisons across sellers is extremely difficult and may remain so.

Health insurance markets today, by and large, are simply not competitive.

Third, entry into health insurance markets is quite difficult. In order to gain market share with a network model plan, insurers must be able to negotiate discounts with providers (and group/staff model plans are in decline). However, providers are often unwilling to negotiate such discounts for carriers with small enrollment. As a consequence, entering a market is very difficult, or doing so requires operating at a loss for some time.

Fourth, insurance industry profits have continued to grow over time, another indication of noncompetitive markets. The analysis by Robinson found that between 2000 and 2003, private insurance revenue increased even faster than medical costs, indicating that insurer market power allowed the firms to not only pass on rising health care costs to purchasers but to also increase profits at the same time. Between 2000 and 2007, annual increases in single and family premiums were 8.9 and 9.5 percent, respectively, while health care spending by the privately insured increased by 6.7 percent. Analysts at Health Care for America Now researched Security and Exchange [Commission] filings and reported large increases in insurance company profits over the same period. And finally, it is very apparent that insurers have considerable flexibility in setting premium rates in the vast majority of markets. As a consequence, those shopping for coverage may be offered different prices for similar products with different carriers, and competition is not driving them to comparable levels. For example, an analysis of how individuals in less-than-perfect health fare in the individual health insurance market found that premium offers for the same individual in the same insurance market could vary across carriers by a factor of 2 to 1 or more. . . .

The Consequences of the Lack of Competitive Markets

Both health insurance markets and provider markets, particularly hospitals, do not meet the conditions for competitive markets. Consolidation has meant there are limited numbers of insurers and providers in many markets. The products offered by sellers in insurance and hospital markets are complex and difficult to understand and evaluate. It is almost impossible to compare prices of either insurance products or services provided by hospitals and other health providers. The barriers to entry in both markets are great. Insurer consolidation means high levels of profitability. While much of the hospital sector is not-for-profit, lack of competition often means increased revenue devoted to the purchase and diffusion of new and expensive technologies and procedures.

The impact of consolidation on prices depends on conditions in particular markets. In markets where there is little concentration among insurers but a concentrated hospital market, there is no real ability for insurers to negotiate with hospitals. A dominant insurer can do better in obtaining discounts from hospitals but will still have little negotiating power with dominant hospital systems. In some markets, dominant insurers have no incentive to be tough negotiators because they have no significant competitors and the demand for health insurance is not very sensitive to price. Small insurers lack bargaining power with providers and thus cannot compete with larger firms on premiums. And finally, there is no real competition in many hospital markets because smaller hospitals cannot challenge the dominant system on the range of available services (e.g., new technologies). The lack of effective competition and demand-side market power has contributed to the medical arms race and health care costs growing considerably faster than the economy. The problem is the lack of countervailing power, thus, in our view, the need for a public plan. . . .

A Public Plan

There are at least two strong arguments for a competing public plan. The first reason is that there is a strong need for cost containment both to lower the growth in health care costs for all Americans and to lower the cost of providing government subsidies for the purchase of insurance to lower-income people. The public plan would have lower administrative costs than private plans and could establish or negotiate provider payment rates at lower levels than private payers are able or willing to do today. The second reason is that some private insurers have denied claims and delayed payments to individuals with high health care needs as a way to control costs. To achieve high rates of voluntary participation in insurance coverage and to create a sense that a mandate to obtain coverage is fair, all individuals, regardless of health status, should have an insurance option with which they feel comfortable. The public plan would play that role for a significant segment of the population. While reformed insurance markets will limit the current ability of private insurers to avoid the sick, in practice, oversight will not be perfect and thus regulations will not be perfectly enforced.

> *Both health insurance markets and provider markets, particularly hospitals, do not meet the conditions for competitive markets.*

We suggest that the public plan would look much like the traditional Medicare program but it would differ in certain important ways. We envision it as a national plan that would compete in local or regional exchanges, using local prices. The public plan would be legally and administratively separate from the exchanges. The policies employed by the public plan would be set at the national level but would be adjusted for local costs. We assume that national legislation would establish insurance market rules that would ensure guaranteed issue and modified community rating (e.g., limited age bands), and would prohibit preexisting condition exclusions and benefit riders. All plans, both private and public, would have to abide by these rules.

All of the plans participating within an exchange (and possibly those outside of it), including the public plan, would offer a limited set of insurance packages consistent with standard benefit guidelines determined at the federal level. While the plans would ideally cover the same set of services, they could vary in the levels of cost sharing required. While all plan levels would be open to all interested enrollees, the level of subsidy would be tied to the plan level deemed most appropriate for a particular income group. For example, the lowest-income population would be subsidized to the plan level with little to no cost-sharing requirement. As income increased, subsidies would be tied to plan levels with increasing cost-sharing requirements. . . .

Enrollment in Public Plan Coverage

We believe that, of those enrolled in exchange-based coverage, the public plan will be most attractive to the lowest-income enrollees. We predict that roughly 70 percent of the low-income exchange enrollees (those under 200 percent of the federal poverty level) would choose the public plan, with the likelihood of choosing the public plan falling as income increases, down to about a third of those with incomes of 400 percent of the poverty level and above. The implication of these estimates is that roughly half of the total exchange population would purchase private plans after weighing the somewhat higher premiums in most of the private plan offerings against other features—that is, access and service—and about 47 million would enroll in coverage through the public plan. The public plan would enroll many of the uninsured, about 13 million by our estimates, and a disproportionate share of those who would receive income-related subsidies.

There are at least two strong arguments for a competing public plan.

Private plans would continue to serve about 161 million Americans (including private administration of self-funded plans for large employers), including about 45 million who would purchase private coverage through local or regional exchanges. Today, 177 million people have private coverage, enrolling either as individuals or through employers. Some of those who now have employer coverage and many with non-group coverage would end up in the public plan, but many who are uninsured and some on Medicaid would end up in private plans, either inside or outside the exchange. As a consequence, after reform, we expect private insurance to cover 91 percent of the total number of lives covered by private insurance today. . . .

The Arguments Against the Public Plan

Several arguments are being made in opposition to having a public plan option available to the non-elderly population.

The first is that the public plan will always be favored—that there is no way that Congress would let the public plan fail and would find ways to tilt the playing field in its favor, providing it with advantages not afforded private plans. However, experience with the Medicare program does not support this concern. Indications from the Medicare Advantage experience suggest that, if anything, private plans would most likely be favored over a public plan. For example, Medicare Advantage plans are paid 14 percent more than Medicare fee for service in 2009 for the average beneficiary, clear evidence that traditional Medicare has not always been favored. Moreover, there are administrative hassles associated with enrolling in the traditional Medicare program, since the vast majority of enrollees also must join three additional plans—Medicare Part B, a private prescription drug plan, and private Medigap/supplemental coverage—to obtain comprehensive protection. If one joins a Medicare Advantage plan, it is one-stop shopping: hospital, physician, prescription drugs, and catastrophic coverage are all provided for one premium. Both examples suggest that the political process does not have a tendency to disadvantage private plan options. . . .

Some have argued that the public plan would misuse its market power, which would lead to underpayments to providers as well as access and quality problems. There are several reasons why this is very unlikely to occur. First, as we have suggested, MedPAC [Medicare Payment Advisory Commission] should be given responsibility to monitor and report on the impact of public plan policies in conjunction with those of Medicare and Medicaid; this should give Congress the information it needs to protect providers from the overuse of market power. Second, providers can, do, and will lobby if they believe the rates that they are paid are inadequate. They have been shown to have considerable political power in this regard. Finally, no one would be required to enroll in the public plan; if they believe that rates are low and as a result, access is poor, they can join a competing private plan. This counterbalancing competitive pressure from the private plans would limit how low the provider payment levels would go in the public plan. . . .

Several arguments are being made in opposition to having a public plan option available to the non-elderly population.

Private Insurance Plans

We believe it is highly unlikely that private insurance would be eradicated by competition from a public insurance plan. Some plans would not survive, but the strongest and most efficient would. First, the public plan would not use all of its potential market power for the reasons outlined above. Rates would be determined based on MedPAC analyses and recommendations. Moreover, providers would lobby over the adequacy of rates. Individuals would move from public plans to private plans if public plan rates were inadequate and led to poor access to providers of choice. Thus, there are significant constraints on the ability of a public plan to use all of its market power, driving down rates below reasonable levels.

Second, there is some evidence that private plans are more effective at managing utilization relative to Medicare fee for service. The private sector has developed wellness and disease management programs that have been widely adopted. The Association of Health Insurance Plans has presented data that suggest that private Medicare Advantage plans have had considerable success in reducing utilization. In one study, they found a 34 percent reduction in hospital days and a 17 percent reduction in hospital readmissions. Another study found an 18 percent reduction in hospital days, a 41 percent reduction in readmissions, and a 32 percent reduction in emergency room visits. MedPAC reports that HMOs' [health maintenance organizations'] bids in Medicare Advantage for the average beneficiary were 98 percent of average fee-for-service expenditures, which suggests the ability to compete. Again, it is not that all private plans would survive; those that have profited through positive risk selection but cannot create incentives for the efficient management of health care will be unlikely to do well in a more competitive environment. However, those that manage care effectively and control utilization will survive, as will those that bargain effectively with providers for lower rates. Plans that provide better consumer service and better access to desired providers than the public plan would do well even with somewhat higher premiums. Private plans would also likely become more aggressive in provider negotiations because of the price competition catalyzed by the public plan.

The Benefits of a Public Plan

A public plan would not destroy the private insurance market but would make it more competitive and lead to the benefits associated with competition. Many private plans would remain attractive because of their ability to be responsive to consumer demands and to be innovative in care management. Public plans are attractive because they can offer better access to necessary care for diverse populations, have lower administrative costs, and have strong negotiating power with providers. The presence of both types of plans should make each perform better in a reformed insurance marketplace. Most importantly, faced with competition from a public plan, private alternatives will become more efficient, leading to declines in their own costs. The net effect would be reduced growth in health care costs.

We estimate that the number of people with private coverage would fall from 177 million to 161 million. Many will leave employer coverage, particularly those in small firms, and join the public plan as will many with non-group coverage. But on the other hand, significant numbers of those who are now uninsured and some now on Medicaid would join private plans, either by taking up coverage in large firms outside the exchange or choosing a private plan within the exchange.

A public plan would not destroy the private insurance market but would make it more competitive and lead to the benefits associated with competition.

We estimate that the public plan could provide substantial savings. Private payment rates by commercial insurers are about 30 percent above those rates paid by Medicare. We argue that it would be unnecessary and probably unwise for the public plan to pay Medicare rates. Under the two alternative assumptions we have made, that the public plan would pay Medicare rates plus 20 percent and plus 10 percent, we estimate that the cost of income-related subsidies needed to obtain universal coverage would save between $224.1 billion and $399.8 billion over 10 years. If the public plan can reduce the annual rate of growth, the savings would be still greater. We emphasize that MedPAC should play an important role in deciding on hospital and physician rates paid under the public plan, taking into consideration implications for access to care, physician incomes, and hospital financial well-being.

A Public Health Plan Is Important for Choice

Jacob Hacker and Rahul Rajkumar

Jacob Hacker is the Stanley B. Resor Professor of Political Science at Yale University and a resident fellow at the Institution for Social and Policy Studies. Rahul Rajkumar is a physician at Brigham and Women's Hospital in Boston and a senior advisor to Doctors for America.

The issue sucking up the oxygen in Washington today is whether to have a public health insurance plan compete with private insurers for the business of Americans without secure workplace coverage. Americans overwhelmingly back the idea, President [Barack] Obama strongly supports it, and House Democratic leaders have drafted legislation that shows how it can be done. But the insurance and pharmaceutical lobbies and some medical provider groups have cried foul, and they have found a receptive ear not just among Republicans but also some Democrats who demand that reform be bipartisan, even if they have to cut the heart out of it.

Opponents of the plan paint a dystopian future in which the government takes over American medicine, limiting choice and competition. The claim is demonstrably false: If the public plan option were enacted, most Americans would continue to get private insurance through their employers as they do today, and the public plan would be just one choice offered alongside a menu of private plans. Yet a post-reform world of unraveling choices, runaway costs, and rampant health insecurity could well materialize—if critics get their way and the public plan dies as a health care bill wends its way to passage.

Jacob Hacker and Rahul Rajkumar, "Health Care Deform," *New Republic*, June 30, 2009. Copyright © 2009 by The New Republic, Inc. Reproduced by permission of The New Republic.

A National Insurance Exchange

Fast forward a few years to the first day that this reform bill—signed with much fanfare in the Rose Garden, with a beaming bipartisan coterie—takes effect. The bill's crown jewel is not the public option, but a "national insurance exchange," a benefit clearinghouse that is supposed to sign up private insurers to provide choices to people without workplace insurance. These choices vary based on the region you live in, to reflect the plans in the local market.

In many markets, however, the choices turn out to be roughly as limited as they are today, when the dominant insurer enrolls at least half of privately insured people in 16 states and at least a third in 38 states. The national insurance exchange is meant to create greater competition, but for most of the country, the choice is basically between WellPoint and UnitedHealth—gargantuan for-profit insurers each about the size of Medicare. Yes, there is more than one choice in most areas, but not choices that meaningfully differ from each other, or from what is on offer today.

> *If a public plan option were enacted, most Americans would continue to get private insurance through their employers as they do today.*

Ironically, the problem is worst in the rural areas of the country whose Democratic senators—such as Kent Conrad of North Dakota and Finance Committee Chair Max Baucus of Montana—have been among the Democrats most willing to forsake the public health insurance plan. In these rural areas, one or two dominant insurers hold over 90 percent of the market. (In all of Montana, for example, one insurer has 75 percent of private enrollees.) For people in these parts of the nation, a real choice of health plans is as mythical as unicorns.

A Failed Reform

Equally mythical, it soon becomes clear, are the consumer co-operatives that Conrad and Baucus had backed to attract Republican support. The reform legislation envisioned that these cooperatives would be chartered by the government and owned by consumers—the idea being that a democratically controlled enterprise would be driven not by profit, but by serving the interests of its citizen-owners. But the cooperatives are almost impossible to get off the ground, just as similar consumer-oriented ventures have been in the past. Doctors largely boycott them, insurers undercut them, state politicians argue over them, and federal dollars are woefully insufficient to nurture them. It soon becomes clear that they represent little more than a fig leaf covering a lack of commitment to the basic aim of a public plan: having a tough competitor that forces large insurance companies to bring up their standards and bring down their prices.

Not surprisingly, the premiums that most plans offer within the exchange are just as high as they are today. Without a public plan offering coverage that, estimates project, would be around 25 percent cheaper, the private plans in many markets are free to gouge consumers without much concern about losing business. And without pressure on these plans to control costs, they aren't about to cut back their administrative waste or high profits or excessive executive salaries, much less bargain aggressively with drug companies and hospitals demanding ever higher prices.

Worse, because coverage within the exchange is subsidized for lower-income workers, taxpayers pick up the tab. With the cost of the health care overhaul outstripping projections, national politicians start the difficult process of cutting the initially generous benefit package and focusing public assistance on the neediest within the exchange. Middle-class Americans start wondering what's in reform for them.

Problems Without a Public Plan

Look a little further down the road. It's been three years since the president signed the bill. Despite high hopes, the patchwork of federal and state insurance regulations created by the legislation isn't working. The worst abuses—such as revoking policies of people who thought they were covered after they've run up big medical bills—have largely ended. But private insurers continue to ration care in arbitrary ways that put their profits before patients, and many Americans still can't obtain or afford private insurance that promises them health security. The basic problem is that the regulations stand alone, without the auxiliary precaution of a public health plan whose mission is to improve the quality and cost-effectiveness of care.

Those with chronic conditions or nearing retirement age who are self-employed or work for small businesses are hit hardest. A 59-year-old self-employed man with diabetes, or a 48-year-old single mother with breast cancer who works at a small retailer—these are the sort of people who will fall through the cracks without a public plan available in all parts of the nation. They may qualify for a "hardship exemption" so that they are not compelled to buy insurance under the reform legislation's "individual mandate." But not being forced to buy insurance they can't afford is a poor substitute for having access to a public plan they can afford.

All this hurts not just patients, but also providers. When reform had passed, doctors and hospitals were told they'd be burdened with less paperwork and fewer uninsured patients. And they almost certainly would have—if reform had covered most Americans, reduced billing hassles and administrative overhead, ensured them a stable connection to their patients, and controlled insurance premiums so those patients could stay insured. But without a patient-centered public plan, providers find themselves in the same old binds they faced before.

A Doomed Future

What's more, there's been no meaningful innovation in the way providers get paid to treat most patients. Private insurers continue to use their old models to pay for care—models that reward volume over performance and quantity over quality. And, as a result, costs have risen inexorably, with health care now consuming more than 20 percent of our nation's annual GDP [gross domestic product], putting growing pressure on public and private budgets.

In alarm, national politicians set about slashing medical spending. While federal policy makers have only the bluntest levers to stimulate innovation among private insurers, they have a ready option for controlling their own health care spending: cutting and restructuring payments to providers and hospitals under Medicare, the largest federal health insurance program. But because Medicare covers only around a seventh of Americans, these efforts are swamped out by cost growth in the overall insurance market. And those seventh of Americans, who vote in high numbers, are not happy about the changes in the coverage they depend on.

Without a patient-centered public plan, providers find themselves in the same old binds they faced before.

They're not the only ones. When reform had passed, its architects had proclaimed 2009 the start of the road to universal coverage. But to avoid the road to reform that ran through the creation of a new public plan, they took the nation down a path strewn with potholes, detours, and drop-offs that everyone, in retrospect, would have liked to avoid.

The Need for a Public Plan

How can we avoid this nightmarish future? By getting the debate right in the present. We can start by recognizing that we are already on a course for financial ruin. A health plan that tinkers around the edges will not help. What we need is a big win on health care—and a big win must include a public health insurance plan.

Our future world of restricted options also makes clear that a public plan is about *choice*. People who lack coverage from their employers will have the option of enrolling in the new public plan. They will also be perfectly free to enroll in a variety of private plans. These plans will compete with the public plan on a completely level playing field—both subject to the same rules, both sustaining themselves completely through enrollee premiums and federal premium assistance, both answering to the same regulatory body.

This is a not a radical idea. In many areas of American commerce, private and government programs comfortably co-exist. FHA [Federal Housing Administration]-insured loans and non-FHA loans, Social Security and private pensions, public and private universities—all have long thrived side by side. Each side of the divide has strengths and weaknesses, but in every case the public sector is providing something the private sector cannot: A *backup* that's there if and when you need it; a *benchmark* for private providers; and a *backstop* to make sure costs don't spin out of control. Just as it is comforting to have Social Security in case your 401(k) evaporates or an FHA loan in case your credit score tanks, a new public plan provides an added level of protection against the vicissitudes of an unaccountable insurance market. A public plan is about competition as well as choice.

> What we need is a big win on health care—and a big win must include a public health insurance option.

Even on a level playing field, the public plan will create discipline for private insurers that regulations alone simply cannot. Regulations require extensive monitoring and vigilance—and, as we know from careful study and long experience, private insurers will try to get around these rules. Having a tough public-spirited competitor means that the regulations do not have to do more work than can be expected of even the most nimble and powerful regulator, much less real-world regulators constantly subject to industry pressure, ideological attacks, and budgetary constraints. So, the public plan is about more than choice and competition. It is also about regulatory realism and restraint of the kind that, in other contexts, conservatives generally espouse.

The goal of the public plan isn't to eliminate private insurance, or to put government in charge of American medicine, or any of the other frightening futures that critics have painted. The goal is to create accountability for the public and private sectors alike while ensuring all Americans have affordable quality care. Sure, there will be tensions and difficult questions to resolve. But the alternative, as we've seen, would be far worse.

A Public Option Is Necessary for Security

Paul Waldman

Paul Waldman is a partner in R5 Advisors, a communications consulting firm, and a senior correspondent with the American Prospect.

Health care wonks worth their salt will tell you that the big issue in the current effort to reform our abysmal health care system is cost control. They say if we don't do something to rein in the spiraling cost of health care, it will eventually bankrupt us all. This is also a key argument made by advocates of what has become the ideological fulcrum of the health care reform debate: the public option. Those who want to give Americans the choice of a government insurance plan have talked a lot about the public option's potential to save money over private coverage. And it would—not only because the government could negotiate lower reimbursement rates but because it wouldn't have to spend money on the things that private insurers do, like underwriting (figuring out whom to avoid covering), marketing, multimillion-dollar executive salaries, and of course, profits. Competition from a less expensive public plan would also force private insurers to become more efficient.

That's all true. But for the most part, we haven't heard the best argument for a public option: security. It's what ought to be at the center of this debate, and it's the one thing private insurance companies will never offer.

The single-payer and hybrid systems in place in every other country in the developed world have many admirable features: lower costs, universal coverage, and better health outcomes. But what ought to make us most envious is their security—it's what they have and we desperately need. If you live in Canada or Germany or France or Japan, there are some things you need never fear. You need never fear that your insurance company will tell you it won't cover treatment for your asthma because you had asthma before they signed you up. You need never fear that you will bankrupt your family because of expensive treatments for a serious illness. You need never fear that you will find yourself without coverage after your insurer dropped you or you lost your job. You might fear getting sick, but you won't fear that your life will be destroyed by not being able to pay for getting sick.

The purpose of a private insurance company is to make money, as much money as possible.

In the United States, unless you're over 65, extremely poor, or a veteran—thus, already covered by a government health insurance plan—you do have to fear all that. That's because the central pathology of our deeply pathological health care system is that most of us have no choice but to get health coverage from an entity whose sole reason for being is to take our money and then try to avoid paying for our care when we get sick.

That may sound harsh, but let's be realistic: The purpose of a private insurance company is to make money, as much money as possible. In this, it's like any other business. But insurance is fundamentally different from other businesses. When you buy a soda, you know exactly how much you're paying for it. And when you take your first sip, you know whether you like it or not. If the soda company wanted to give you the shaft, it would only have two ways to do it: It could give you a bad-tasting product or charge you lots of money for it. Either way, you'd only end up buying it once.

But when you buy insurance, you enter into a complex relationship with a company that promises to pay for services you haven't yet used. You start paying it substantial amounts of money right away, but you don't actually use its service until some time in the future. You're also required to sign lengthy, intricate documents full of conditions and exclusions and legalese that few people are equipped to understand. You are at the company's mercy, which makes its incentives and inclinations so important.

As long as most people have no choice but to get coverage through a private insurance company, security is the one thing we won't have.

The private health insurance market is dominated by four gigantic insurers: UnitedHealth, WellPoint, Aetna, and Cigna. In the last five years, companies have combined to earn over $44 billion in profits; UnitedHealth alone has made over $17 billion in profits over that period. "On Wall Street," the *Los Angeles Times* has noted, these companies "showcase their efforts to hold down expenses and maximize shareholder returns by excluding customers likely to need expensive care, including those with chronic diseases such as asthma and diabetes. The companies lobby governments to take over responsibility for their sickest customers so they can reserve the healthiest (and most profitable) for themselves."

And you can see it if you go to their Web sites, each of which contains a photo montage that cycles through as you look at the page. The photos are certainly not of sick people, or even of doctors and nurses performing their duties. They're of healthy people, mostly younger adults, doing things like gamboling through meadows, looking adoringly at their children, and smiling in the deep contentedness that comes from knowing they will never, ever get sick.

Perhaps a reform bill without a public option could regulate the insurance companies enough to keep them from engaging in their most despicable business practices. We could outlaw the practice of rescission (in which they cash your premiums, than kick you off your plan once you get a serious illness). We could make them accept anyone, regardless of preexisting conditions. We could set up an insurance exchange, a kind of managed market where people could easily compare different plans and have a variety of choices. As part of the deal for getting access to this pool of customers, we could force the insurers to accept "community rating"—charging everyone within a population the same price, no matter their age, gender, or medical history. Those regulations would certainly go a long way toward curbing the worst abuses.

Call me cynical, but I can't help but assume that even if we do all that, the insurance companies will still come up with a dozen creative new ways to cut people off, avoid paying claims, and generally pad their profits at the expense of their enrollees' health and security. There's a reason why they'll fight against the public option with every ounce of strength—and every dollar—they can muster (insurance companies spent $74 million on lobbyists in 2008 alone). It's because the presence of a plan that offers security is a dire threat to their business model. It's possible that the health care system could be improved without a public option. But as long as most people have no choice but to get coverage through a private insurance company, security is the one thing we won't have.

A Public Option Would Worsen the Health Care System

Frank S. Rosenbloom

Frank S. Rosenbloom is a physician and president of Oregon Right to Life.

The health care debate in this country is an old story. It began in 1934 when President Franklin D. Roosevelt attempted to include government-funded health care in his "New Deal" as part of his comprehensive Social Security legislation. President Roosevelt was very concerned that the Supreme Court might rule parts of his "New Deal" unconstitutional. He tried to induce Congress to approve increasing the total number of justices on the Supreme Court to fifteen, attempting thereby to circumvent the judiciary and the Constitution by stacking the Court in his favor.

Government Intervention in Health Care

Subsequently, government-funded health care has been debated in nearly every session of Congress since 1939.

Many people assume that the establishment of Medicare in 1965 was the result solely of Lyndon Johnson's Great Society legislation. In fact, the establishment of Medicare was the culmination of decades of efforts by progressive liberals and was seen as a stepping-stone to government-funded health care for all. In fact, some of the tactics the government used to pass Medicare were illegal at the time, employing taxpayer money to lobby for political programs.

Today President [Barack] Obama theorizes that a government "option" will increase competition, lower costs, and provide better medical care for larger numbers of people. In any scientific endeavor, the veracity of a theory is determined by whether it is supported by empirical evidence and predictive of future outcomes. Therefore, we must examine Obama's assertions in light of the available evidence.

Every time the government has gotten involved in health care, competition has been suppressed by practices that would be prosecutable if carried out by private companies.

The Public Option and Competition

1. A government health care option will increase competition.

In order to determine whether this is the case, we must review whether government involvement has ever increased competition in the past. We must remember that the force of law attends government involvement and that the force of law gives an advantage to the government. For instance, Medicare and Medicaid employ price-fixing, which is illegal for any private organization. The government decides on the worth of medical services and the providers of those services must comply. The government therefore utilizes unfair practices to establish a monopoly, transferring costs to the private sector, artificially magnifying the cost of private insurance and hiding the true cost of government coverage.

When Medicare was passed, senior citizens were promised that Medicare would not prevent them from utilizing private primary insurance if they wanted to. This assurance was false. Private primary health insurance has become all but impossible for persons over 65 to obtain.

Medicaid recipients, as well as those on military health plans, are significantly restricted in their choices. This lack of choice has stifled competition. Contrary to the claims of the current administration, every time government has gotten involved in health care, competition has been suppressed by practices that would be prosecutable if carried out by private companies. Far from promoting competition, a government plan will eventually eliminate private health care, thereby eliminating all competition.

Tom Miller, director of Health Policy Studies at the Cato Institute [from 2000–2003], explained:

> "As fiscal pressures mount, the federal government does not 'negotiate' with medical providers for lower prices for covered services. It dictates below-market reimbursements with its near-monopoly power as a purchaser of health care for seniors. The full costs of such price discounts eventually reduce access to quality care and hold health care markets hostage to political exploitation."

Government Intervention and Cost

2. A government option will decrease costs.

It is naïve to believe that increased government intervention will lower the cost of medicine. All past evidence indicates that the reverse is true. In 1965, the government promised that Medicare Part A would cost $9 billion by 1990. The actual cost was more than $66 billion—over seven times projected costs. There has *never* been a single large federal social program that has come in at budget or has performed as predicted.

Once the government has a monopoly . . . the government will do what it has always done: use its power to ration services and increase taxes.

Democrats have tried to pin the rising cost of medical care on the private sector. It is, however, government interference and government regulations that have caused the high cost of medical care in the past and that will continue to increase the costs of medical care in the future. Medicare increases the cost of medical care by shifting federal administrative overhead to the private sector and through oppressive regulation. . . .

The estimated $1.6 trillion for Obama's proposed legislation will cover only about one-third of his claimed 45 million uninsured. If historical precedents and evidence are any indication, the actual costs of the plan could be seven times higher than this estimate. Adding to the fiscal nightmare, Mr. Obama is planning on cutting benefits for Medicare and Medicaid in order to transfer funding to his new health plan. This is another example that government does not contain costs, but shifts costs from one program to another.

The effect of Obama's program will be to increase taxes on small businesses and further worsen unemployment. This loss of jobs will result in driving people into the government-funded plan. Increasing the costs of the plan would create a vicious cycle of unemployment, increasing costs, rising taxes, and unending dependence on government.

A Government Monopoly

3. A government option will improve health care and cover more people.

Mr. Obama's claim of 45 million Americans without medical insurance is completely unfounded. His health care plan will initially cover about 13 million people. However, nearly 100 million people will be eligible for the proposed government option. As mentioned above, nothing about the plan would promote increased competition.

Once the government has a monopoly on all health care in America and the costs to the government have skyrocketed, the government will do what it has always done: use its power to ration services and increase taxes. This will result in inferior medical care for the American people.

Once this rationing occurs, there will be no turning back. The government will be in complete control, as it is with

Medicare and Medicaid. We need only ask Medicare or VA [Department of Veterans Affairs] patients about the difficulties they face in trying to obtain payments for their medical care to understand what the end result will be. Denial of payment for care is simply rationing by another name. Furthermore, the evidence shows that government-funded health care initiated at the state level, such as the programs in Massachusetts and Oregon, have failed miserably. We will likely have to consider the morgue as an integral part of any government health care system in the future.

Albert Einstein once defined insanity as doing the same thing over and over again expecting different results. Mr. Obama's theories are undeniably refuted by historical fact, and therefore his projections are unreliable and even dangerous. There is overwhelming evidence that his health care plan will result in a fiscal and medical care disaster. More important, his plan would result in a wider unconstitutional expansion of government control over our lives. We must demand real solutions, not the trading of unsustainable benefits for votes, the loss of our liberty, and greater dependence for our medical care—not on those trained in the healing arts—but on government and professional politicians.

A Public Option Will Not Increase Competition and Choice

Jeff Jacoby

Jeff Jacoby is a columnist for the Boston Globe.

"My guiding principle is and always has been that consumers do better when there is choice and competition." So said President [Barack] Obama in his address to Congress on health care, making an argument for a government-run "public option" to sell health insurance that many Democrats have echoed.

In 34 states, Obama noted, three-fourths of the insurance market is controlled by five or fewer companies. "Without competition, the price of insurance goes up and the quality goes down." But add a public option "administered by the government just like Medicaid or Medicare," he said, and competition would revive.

No, it wouldn't.

A government-run health insurer would radically tilt the health insurance playing field. It would amount to a new entitlement program, able to undercut the price of private insurance by squeezing hospitals and doctors, reimbursing them at below-market rates. "Just like Medicaid and Medicare," which also underpay medical providers, the public option would force hospitals and doctors to charge private insurers more. Insurers would be compelled to raise their premiums, eventually losing millions of customers to the government plan.

Obama insists that any public option would have to be self-supporting, properly balancing its premiums and risk and

Jeff Jacoby, "An Option for Public: Less Government, More Choice," *Boston Globe*, November 4, 2009. Copyright © 2009 Boston Globe. Reproduced by permission.

not expecting the government to cover its losses. Sound familiar? The same assurances were made about Fannie Mae and
Freddie Mac.

"I have no interest in putting insurance companies out of
business," the president says. As a US Senate candidate in
2003, he sang a different tune: "I happen to be a proponent of
a single-payer universal health care program. . . . But as all of
you know, we may not get there immediately." Has he changed
his mind? Or only his talking points?

---

*A government-run health insurer would radically tilt the
health insurance playing field.*

More competition among health insurers is a consumma-
tion to be devoutly wished. But there are better ways to get
there than a public option.

Here are three:

- *Tear down the barriers to buying insurance across state
  lines.* Under federal law, states are permitted to regulate
  "the business of insurance" as they see fit, and most
  have seen fit to allow the sale only of insurance policies
  licensed by their own insurance commissions. As a consequence, there is no competitive national market for
  health insurance; there are 50 state markets instead,
  most of which are dominated by a handful of insurers.
  This, says Michael [F.] Cannon of the Cato Institute, is
  the "original sin" of health insurance regulation.

When it comes to almost any other product or service,
Americans would find a ban on interstate commerce and competition intolerable: Imagine being told that you could buy a
car only if it was manufactured in your state. Consumers in
the market for a mortgage are free to do business with an
out-of-state lender; those in the market for health insurance
should be equally free to do business with an out-of-state insurer.

- *Repeal mandatory benefits that make health insurance needlessly expensive.* Compounding the lack of interstate competition is the way states drive up the cost of health insurance by making certain types of coverage compulsory. Consumers and insurers should be free to work out for themselves just how comprehensive or limited a policy should be. But state mandates prevent such flexibility by requiring insurance companies to sell a fixed array of benefits that many customers may not want. Individuals seeking plain-vanilla health insurance—a policy that will cover them, say, in case of major surgery or catastrophic illness—may find themselves forced to pay for a policy that also covers acupuncture, in vitro fertilization, alcoholism therapy, and a dozen additional treatments.

When compulsion takes the place of competition, the result is invariably less choice at higher cost.

- *De-link health insurance from employment.* Nothing distorts America's health insurance market like the misbegotten tax preference for employer-sponsored health insurance. Until that preference is removed, millions will continue to rely on their employers' health plans, rather than buying insurance for themselves. Fix the tax code, and no longer could insurance companies routinely bypass employees and deal only with their employers. Instead we would see intense competition for individual customers—and the lower premiums such competition would yield.

Yes, Mr. President, consumers *do* benefit from choice and competition. The key to both is not more government regulation and control, but less.

CHAPTER 4

How Should the
American Health Care
System Be Reformed?

Overview: American Health Care Reform

Scott Bittle and Jean Johnson

Scott Bittle is director of public issues analysis, and Jean Johnson is director of education insights and director of programs at Public Agenda, a public opinion research organization.

We've all heard friends and coworkers say, 'I can't afford to get sick.' For many, this isn't just about meeting a deadline at work or school. Millions of Americans worry about whether they can pay their medical bills, or whether they can get care at all. Even those with good health insurance worry about the bureaucracy and complexity of the system.

The U.S. Health Care System

Consider these facts:

- What the average person pays for insurance premiums and out-of-pocket costs rose by 50 percent between 2000 and 2005, from an average of $6,200 to $9,100 per person.

- Some 47 million Americans, nearly 16 percent of the population, don't have health insurance at all.

- Unpaid medical bills are the nation's leading cause of personal bankruptcy.

- Our country's total health care bill is projected to hit $4.3 trillion by 2017 and account for about one-fifth of the total economy. That's double the $2.1 trillion we spent in 2006.

Health care costs in the United States are hurting individuals, government and businesses. What makes this problem harder to solve is that there isn't just one cause behind it. There are a lot of reasons for these astronomical sums, including:

Technological advances. Science keeps coming up with new cures, which is wonderful—and expensive.

An aging population. As 78 million baby boomers hit retirement age, they're going to be subject to the extra medical needs everyone faces as they get older.

Millions of Americans worry about whether they can pay their medical bills, or whether they can get care at all.

It's hard for most people to tell how much their health care really costs. Most people who have insurance only pay part of the cost through co-pays, deductibles or employee contributions—the insurance company pays the rest, and the patient may or may not ever see a bill. And since different insurance plans negotiate different deals with providers, the bills for two people with the same illness could be quite different. Many experts say that since the patient isn't bearing the real cost, there's no incentive to control costs.

General inefficiency. Since the U.S. health care system isn't really a single system but a combination of private insurance plans and government programs, that means different forms and different rules for every situation. (The United States spends more than $400 billion a year in health care paperwork, more than three times per capita what Canada spends.) Some experts blame factors like high compensation for health care companies and providers and medical malpractice lawsuits.

Unhealthy lifestyles. Americans may not be taking good enough care of themselves, with rising obesity rates and falling exercise levels.

Private and Public Health Care Spending

The United States spends far more per capita on health care than any other nation, and yet some critics argue Americans aren't getting their money's worth. Despite tremendous gains in health and average longevity, from 47 to 77 years since 1900, measures of U.S. medical well-being lag behind those of several dozen other nations. (Japanese life expectancy, for example, is nearly five years longer than Americans'.) A RAND Corporation study found that only half of the treatments that Americans receive are considered 'best practices.'

Most Americans (about six in 10) get their health coverage as an employee benefit. As a result, the number of uninsured people tends to swing up and down with the economy, as employers lay off or cut back in hard times. Low-income people and young adults are most likely to be uninsured. Those without insurance are 25 percent more likely to die during any given year than those with insurance. And of course, even though people with employer-provided insurance only pay a fraction of their health costs, it's far from free—the Kaiser Family Foundation reports the average family premium is more than $12,000 per year, of which employees pay roughly one-quarter. The government does play a major role in providing health care, through programs for the elderly (Medicare), the poor (Medicaid) and low-income children, as well as through veterans benefits and insurance for federal employees and their families.

There are many ideas about how to improve the American health care system.

In fact, the federal government currently pays for about 45 percent of the nation's health care bills. The government also provides substantial tax breaks ($225 billion total) for employers who provide insurance. People who aren't covered by an employer or the government can still buy health coverage from an insurance company on their own—but relatively few do. Individuals end up paying the highest rates, because businesses usually negotiate a cheaper group rate.

So this makes the rising cost of health care a challenge for government, business and families alike. Businesses are increasingly worried about the cost to their bottom line. General Motors, for example, says it spent $5.6 billion covering its 1.1 million employees in 2006, and claims health costs added $1,500 to the sticker price of every car it makes. While very few businesses said they intended to drop health benefits in 2008, one in five said they were likely to raise employee premiums, according to a Kaiser Family Foundation survey.

For the government, health care costs may become a budget-buster. The combination of the aging baby boom generation and rising costs makes Medicare the most worrisome part of the federal budget. Medicare spending will be about $400 billion in 2008. Medicaid and children's health spending will be around $216 billion, and state Medicaid costs are likely to be about $160 billion. All of these numbers are projected to double within a decade. But controlling costs brings up fundamental questions of fairness. Few topics are as potentially controversial as setting limits on health care. When managed care companies became popular in the 1990s, there was intense debate over their attempts to control costs and approve procedures. Yet some limits may well be needed if we're going to control costs.

Three Different Directions

There are many ideas about how to improve the American health care system—and frankly it's going to take a while to really make sense of the situation and fix all the problems Americans complain about. But here are three different directions a lot of politicians talk about, directions the country might move in.

Choice One: It's time for a single national health insurance system—basically let's have Medicare for everyone.

The big plus is that everyone would have insurance and the money now going to insurance companies and their profits could actually be spent on health care.

The big risk is that this would be monumentally expensive and give a big government agency the power to say what kind of care will be covered and what won't.

Choice Two: It's time to use competition and the power of the marketplace to bring down costs and give people more choices.

The big plus is that people would have many more choices for the kinds of insurance they want and competition among insurers for your business would make the policies more affordable.

The big risks are that insurers would take advantage of the situation and that most people really need help deciding which policies will be best.

Choice Three: The best thing to do is to have all employers provide health insurance for their workers and to have government help people who aren't working buy it on their own.

The big plus is that this builds on our current system and keeps most of the health care system in the private sector—not in the hands of government.

The big risk is that this basically expands a system that is astronomically expensive and confusing—it does very little to squeeze the duplication and excess out of the system.

Single-Payer Health Care Is the Best Option

Don McCanne

Don McCanne is a senior health policy fellow at Physicians for a National Health Program.

L et's begin with the basic premise that our health care financing system should ensure that everyone receives the health care that they need without having to face a financial hardship. Everyone agrees that we have a very expensive system that falls far short of this goal, so it needs to be reformed.

The Compromise Model

The enthusiasm for the model of reform described by Jacob Hacker and endorsed by the Health Care for America NOW (HCAN) coalition, which Jonathan Cohn wrote about in his recent *New Republic* piece "Single-Minded," is understandable. It is a model that attempts to align policy with politics, allegedly meeting the previously unattainable threshold of feasibility. But is it feasible, and will it even work?

Superficially, the model seems to be a workable compromise between those who believe that markets should provide health care coverage through competing private health plans, giving more control to the individual, and those who believe that a government insurance program would be more efficient and effective in ensuring that everyone has adequate health care coverage. Those on the right can support the private plans, and those on the left can purchase the competing public, Medicare-like program. Those in the middle can decide which model would become more prevalent, so goes the theory.

Don McCanne, "Disputations: Is Single-Payer Health Care the Best Option?" *New Republic*, July 16, 2008. Copyright © 2008 by The New Republic, Inc. Reproduced by permission of The New Republic.

Anyone who really believes in this model understands that the private insurance plans would have to be very tightly regulated to reduce the profound deficiencies in our current insurance markets. The current private insurance business model depends on selling the insurers' products to the large numbers of us who are healthy, especially the healthy workforce and their healthy families, while avoiding the need to contribute to the risk pools that cover those who have greater health care needs. Those costs are largely passed on to taxpayers through government programs.

The Lack of Affordability

Other nations that use private plans require effective pooling between plans through various regulatory mechanisms, reducing the problem of adverse selection and ensuring that premiums or taxes are adequate to pay for the care for those with greater needs. Even if the pools are nominally segregated, they function more like a universal risk pool through mechanisms such as risk adjustment and post-claims inter-insurance transfers.

The United States has a unique problem that would make it much more difficult to require private insurers to participate in a quasi-universal risk pool. On a per capita basis, we pay far more for health care than do other nations. Average-income individuals in other nations that use private plans can still afford premiums (or their tax equivalents). In those countries, only low-income individuals require some form of government subsidy for their care.

Compare that with the United States. For healthy risk pools, such as those of employer-sponsored plans, premiums are no longer affordable for average-income individuals and families, whether paid directly by the insured, or nominally by the employer. Imagine a tightly regulated insurance market that ended adverse selection and required benefits at a level that would prevent financial hardship for those with health care needs. The private insurers would find it absolutely impossible to provide us with compliant products that had affordable premiums.

The Failure of the Private Insurance Model

Because of our very high costs, we must accept the fact that the insurance function is no longer simply a transfer from the many who are healthy to the fewer with health care needs, but it now must also include a partial transfer from the wealthy to middle- and lower-income individuals with needs. There is no alternative to this wealth transfer, and that alone creates doubt as to whether a model of highly regulated private plans is politically feasible.

How would that transfer take place in a premium-based system? If the premium were based on income, the premiums that wealthier individuals would have to pay would be so high that it would be a non-starter. Also, we already have a system with burdensome administrative costs. Adding more administration for the purpose of adjusting premiums to match incomes would add to that burden.

We have to get over the idea that financing should be through premiums set by the actuarial value of the benefits in the insurance products. Those premiums are no longer affordable for most of us, and the complexities of income-related adjustments, whether through premium adjustments or tax credits, create an administrative nightmare. It is time that we separate the financing of the universal risk pool from the health care benefit package. The tax system provides us with the most equitable and efficient method of financing our global health care costs.

Perhaps a more compelling reason that the private insurance model no longer works is that it is very ineffective in slowing the increases in health care costs, and everyone agrees that affordability is now a major problem. Most of the current political cost-saving proposals would have very little impact on total costs. We need to address the true major cost drivers: the profound administrative excesses, the lack of an adequate primary care infrastructure, the waste of non-beneficial high-tech excesses, and the lack of a rational system of health care pricing. Even in a regulated environment, it would be very difficult for a multitude of private insurers and public programs to have much impact on these excess costs. Most economists agree that a monopsony, or single purchaser of health care products and services, would be most effective in extracting value through a negotiated realignment of incentives in our health care purchasing.

The Feasibility Dispute

So why don't we just give up, let the private insurance market continue as is, and provide tax subsidies for those who need them, and then offer the single-payer holdouts a public program to make them happy? The problem is that you would fail to gain the efficiencies and equities of the single-payer model if the public program is only another option in the insurance market. It alone would not have enough purchasing power to negotiate optimal value. The public option surely would be subject to adverse selection and sink of its own weight.

The tax system provides us with the most equitable and efficient method of financing our global health care costs.

So where are we on feasibility? The insurance industry wants only the healthy to ensure the success of their business model while passing much of the costs of health care on to the taxpayers. The conservatives do not want a public Medicare-like option for fear of gradual transformation into a single-payer system. Many liberals do not want a free market private insurance system, but rather want private plans to be so tightly regulated that they almost function like a single-payer system, though using private plans is the most expensive model of universal coverage.

This debate that is taking place within the progressive community is missing the center of the feasibility dispute. It is implied that the Hacker/HCAN progressive model would be just fine if the single-payer advocates would come to their senses and join in. It ignores the fact that this model is simply not politically feasible: It loses the support of market enthusiasts because of its dependency on tight regulatory control, intrusion by a government insurance program, and the necessity of a massive infusion of tax funds.

The Single-Payer Model

If you are going to accept that those changes are necessary to provide adequate coverage for everyone, then you might as well go ahead and establish a much more efficient and effective single-payer national health program. Some may argue that explicit calls for income transfer and bureaucratic control of spending are what limit the political feasibility of the single-payer model, but the private plans/public option model would have to incorporate the same principles, and their advocates should be very frank about that up front.

> *We need the truly beneficial disruptive innovation of replacing the obsolete model of private plans with an efficient single-payer national health program.*

HCAN has rejected the single-payer model as not being feasible because it is too disruptive. Yet their model turns the insurance industry upside down, and places the government in the dominant role. Isn't that disruptive? Besides, aren't many of the advances that we see in the technical world today due to disruptive innovations? New, improved, lower-cost technology replaces older, less effective and more expensive technology. That is certainly disruptive to the firms whose products are replaced. But isn't disruptive innovation precisely what we need in health care financing today?

What we don't need is the feeble disruption of the old model of private health insurance by retaining it and modifying it to try to make it work in our very expensive health care environment. We need the truly beneficial disruptive innovation of replacing the obsolete model of private plans with an efficient single-payer national health program.

So, the bottom line? We need reform that provides everyone the health care that they need, without financial barriers that would impede access. We can attempt to maneuver around the ubiquitous mines and trap doors of the political common ground of Hacker/HCAN, and still end up short if we survive. Or we can go straight to a proven model that would accomplish all of our financing goals—a single-payer national health program.

A Single-Payer National Health Program Is Not the Best Option

Ezekiel J. Emanuel

Ezekiel J. Emanuel is a special advisor for health policy to the director of the White House Office of Management and Budget, and head of the Department of Bioethics at the Clinical Center of the National Institutes of Health.

Many liberals in America dream about single-payer plans. Even if they acknowledge that a single-payer plan cannot be enacted, they still think it the best reform. Another proposal may be politically necessary to achieve universal coverage, but it would be a compromise, a fallback. Single payer is the ideal.

This is wrong. Even in theory, single payer is not the best reform option. Here's the problem: while it proposes the most radical reform of the health care financing system, it is conservative, even nostalgic, when it comes to the broken delivery system. It retains and solidifies the nineteenth-century, fragmented, fee-for-service delivery system that provides profligate and bad quality care.

Problems with the Delivery System

Reform of the American health care system needs to address problems with both the financing and the delivery systems. As proponents of single-payer systems note, the financing system is inequitable, inefficient, and unsustainable. There are now forty-seven million uninsured Americans, about 70 percent of whom are in families with full-time workers. Wealthy indi-

Ezekiel J. Emanuel, "The Problem with Single-Payer Plans," *Hastings Center Report*, vol. 38, January-February, 2008, p. 38–41. Copyright © 2008 Hastings Center. Reproduced by permission.

viduals receive much higher tax breaks than the poor, and insurance premiums are a larger percent of wages for those working at low wages and in small businesses. Many working poor and lower middle-class Americans pay taxes to support Medicaid and SCHIP [State Children's Health Insurance Program], yet are excluded from these programs. The employer-based and individual market parts of the financing system are inefficient because they have huge administrative costs, especially related to insurance underwriting, sales, and marketing. The government part of the finance system is inefficient because it fails to address key policy issues, fraud, and—for Medicaid—complex determinations of eligibility. Over the last three decades, health care costs have risen 2–4 percent over growth in the overall economy. Medicaid is now the largest part of state budgets, forcing states to cut other programs.

Even in theory, single payer is not the best reform option.

But the delivery system is also fraught with problems. First, it is badly fragmented. Currently, 75 percent of physicians practice in groups of eight or less. Of the one billion office visits each year, one-third are to solo practitioners, and one-third are to groups of four or fewer physicians. On average, each year Medicare beneficiaries see seven different physicians, who are financially, clinically, and administratively uncoordinated.

A second problem is that the delivery system is structured for acute care, but the contemporary need is for chronic care. Over 133 million Americans have chronic conditions, and among Americans sixty-five and older, 75 percent have two or more chronic conditions, and 20 percent have five chronic conditions. Consequently, 70 percent of health care costs are devoted to patients with chronic conditions.

Also, the care that the system delivers is of much poorer quality than Americans realize. Use of unproven, non-beneficial, marginal, or harmful services is common. The list of offending interventions that are paid for and widely used but either unproven or of marginal benefit to patients is vast— IMRT [intensity-modulated radiation therapy] and proton beam for early prostate cancer, CT [computer tomography] and MRI [magnetic resonance imaging] angiograms, Epogen for chemotherapy induced anemia, Erbitux and Avastin for colorectal cancer, and drug-eluting stents for coronary artery disease. Stanford researchers recently showed that between 15 and 20 percent of prescriptions are written for indications for which there is absolutely no published data supporting their use. The Dartmouth studies on variation in practices demonstrate that for many interventions, more services are not better. For instance, heart attack patients in Miami receive vastly more care than similar patients in Minnesota at 2.45 times the cost, yet have slightly worse outcomes.

The Benefits of a Single-Payer Plan

In the context of reforming the American health care system, "single payer" has come to be associated with three key reforms: *a single national plan* for all Americans, *reduced administrative costs*, and *negotiated prices* for hospitals and physicians and perhaps for health care goods and services, such as drugs. Single-payer plans have two huge advantages.

First, single-payer plans clearly provide for universal health care coverage. Unlike Massachusetts-style individual mandate reform proposals, single-payer plans do not achieve 95 percent or 97 percent coverage, but true 100 percent coverage for all Americans.

Second, single-payer plans enhance the efficiency of the health care financing system by eliminating the wasteful costs of insurance underwriting, sales, and marketing. This could save between $60 and $100 billion. Similarly, a single-payer plan with a formulary and negotiated prices would be able to reduce drug costs. McKinsey Global Institute has estimated that bringing drug costs in the United States down to those of other developed countries would save the U.S. system $57 billion. This is a huge and real savings, enough to cover all the uninsured and probably expand the range of covered services to include dental care and other items.

The problem with single-payer plans is that they have an assortment of serious structural problems. . . .

The Problem of Fee for Service

Single-payer plans would preserve the dysfunctional delivery system. We know two things about how to reform the delivery system. First, because no one yet has the secret formula for delivering the best quality health care, a real reform of the financing system needs to foster innovation in delivery and then measure the delivery system to find out what changes improve quality. Second, while the overall contours of reform are unknown, there is a clear need for better integration and coordination of care. Integration requires three I's— infrastructure, information, and incentives. Better delivery of care needs an infrastructure that coordinates doctors, hospitals, home health care agencies, and other providers administratively, fiscally, and clinically. They need to share information easily. And there have to be incentives for this coordination. It will not happen spontaneously.

The problem with single-payer plans is that they have an assortment of serious structural problems.

The problem is that a single-payer approach uses fee-for-service reimbursement to entrench the existing delivery system. Retaining and institutionalizing the fee-for-service payment model would quash the ability to integrate care. Solo practitioners or small groups would have no incentive—financial or otherwise—for integration and coordination of care across providers.

Also, single-payer reform is hostile to the very organizations that have the financial and administrative capacity to build the infrastructure and information systems for the coordinated care delivery systems: insurance companies and health plans. If there is to be an infrastructure for integration of services, information sharing, and incentives for collaboration, some organization has to develop and implement it. Call it what you will, that organization would look a lot like a health insurance company. (Some might argue that the [Department of] Veterans Affairs [VA] health system is a single-payer system that does a great job of coordinating and integrating care. True, but it covers only thirteen million people. In essence, the VA is a big health plan, like Kaiser [Permanente]. There is no way a single administrative body can efficiently coordinate care for three hundred million people.) In the current system, the financial incentives for health insurance companies lead to perverse behaviors, such as avoiding sick patients. But single-payer plans eliminate not only their problems, but also their potential benefits.

The Problem of Deceptive Administrative Savings

There is no doubt that a single-payer system would produce huge administrative savings, but low administrative costs should not be confused with low total health care costs.

Very low administrative costs in Medicare create an opening for fraud and abuse. The last assessment by the Inspector General [IG] of the Department of Health and Human Services occurred in 1996. At that time, the IG estimated that Medicare made about $23.2 billion in improper payments due to insufficient or absent documentation, incorrect billing, billing for excluded services, and other problems. In 1996, Medicare spent about $200 billion. Thus, fraud was over 10 percent of total Medicare costs. (I leave it to you to imagine why the government has not repeated this assessment in the last decade.) True, the Canadian single-payer system does not report high levels of fraud and abuse, but Canada is not the United States. Canada's population is about one-tenth that of the United States, and Canadians believe in good government.

Furthermore, a plan covering all Americans would be much larger than Medicare. It would have to process more than one billion physician visits, forty million hospitalizations, and 3.7 billion prescriptions each year. This would require sophisticated information technology, but that technology would be a major administrative cost, and keeping it updated could be politically difficult. As we have seen in the IRS [Internal Revenue Service] and the FBI [Federal Bureau of Investigation], there is great aversion to spending money on major IT [information technology] upgrades.

Finally, monitoring the quality of care delivered to patients also constitutes an administrative expense. It is an administrative burden to systematically assess whether new technologies like cancer genetic fingerprints are in fact beneficial, whether new surgical procedures really lead to longer life, and whether new ways of preparing patients for surgery and handling intravenous lines reduce infections and hospital days.

A plan covering all Americans would be much larger than Medicare.

Nothing would absolutely prohibit single-payer plans from spending more money on administration to detect fraud, improve computerization, address payment issues, and assess quality. Nothing, that is, but a strong ideological commitment to keeping administrative expenses very, very low. The war cry for single-payer plans is very low administrative costs, but repeatedly touting this advantage creates a line in the sand. Indeed, it may exacerbate the inflexibility of a single-payer plan. Because of its size, any agency administering a single-payer plan would have a built-in tendency toward inertia. Further, striving to keep administrative costs low would translate into hiring fewer people to manage the system. Fewer people would mean less expertise for addressing problems and less time to search for creative solutions. This is a prescription for inflexibility and lack of innovation.

The Problem of Controlling Costs

Efficiency savings from reduced administrative costs or cheaper drug prices should not be confused with controlling costs overall. Efficiencies, such as reducing administrative waste, are one-time savings. *Controlling costs* means reducing the increase in medical spending year after year. Single-payer plans use the savings from efficiencies to extend coverage to the uninsured and expand covered services without raising the total amount spent on health care. But these one-time savings do not attack the fundamental forces that drive health care cost inflation. Unless there is some mechanism to control those pressures, the one-time savings would be used up in a few years, and overall health care spending would go higher and higher. How can single-payer plans respond to this health care inflation?

There are three possible approaches. One is to "constrain the supply": use the national health plan's control to constrain the introduction and deployment of technology. A single-payer plan could decide to limit the number of MRI scanners, for example. Indeed, in the Physicians' Working Group proposal, the national health plan would negotiate with hospitals on capital expansion and could easily limit how many hospitals can build facilities for MRI scanners or new specialized surgical suites. This strategy creates queuing for access to the technology. As every major country trying this has learned, queuing creates huge public resentment. People on the waiting list get furious at the central administration. Americans, especially the upper middle class, are unlikely to tolerate it.

Constraining supply also promotes gaming of the system and inequality. When technology is limited, patients—and physicians—try to jump the queue. Physicians are not great at creating priority lists based on medical need. Particularly when they have their own practices, their obligation is to their individual patients, not to ensuring that other physicians' patients get care and not to promoting the overall health of the population.

Countries that have tried this approach have found, not surprisingly, that such gaming tends to favor well-off patients. In many facets of life, well-off people have learned how to come out on top in situations where there are limits. Limits on health care technology gives them one more setting in which their greater gaming skills can be deployed. A study in Winnipeg, Canada, showed that although all Canadians were legally entitled to the same services, the well off had substantially better access to high-technology services that were constrained.

The Danger of Lower Prices and Fees

A second approach, a variant of "constrain the supply," is a "low prices and fees" approach. As the only organization paying physicians, hospitals, drug companies, and other health providers, a national health plan would have a huge incentive to squeeze down on fees. This would keep costs down, and since providers would have no one else to turn to, they would have limited recourse.

The United States government uses this low-price approach in Medicaid and Medicare. To save money, every so often Congress or the Medicare administrators roll back the fees paid to hospitals, physicians, and others. Then, just as predictably, those groups scream that they are going broke and lobby Congress to increase the fees. And so the seesaw goes on— prices rolled back and then increased after lobbying. This does not end up saving much, in part because how much is paid out depends not only on the fee or price but also on the volume—on how much is done. So one way physicians respond to lower fees is to ramp up volume; they see a lot of patients for shorter and shorter times. This is easily done because for many diseases there are no data on how often patients should be seen in the physician's office. And it is exactly how Canadian health insurance administrators kept fees low.

When technology is limited, patients—and physicians— try to jump the queue.

The British National Health Service used to do exactly what the Physicians' Working Group wants to do: It paid hospitals a fixed price for operating expenses and controlled capital expenditures to limit expansion and the purchase of new technologies. The result: The hospitals put off maintenance and began falling apart. They put off cleaning and became filthy. They could not buy new equipment or adapt quickly to changes in medical practice. Eventually, even the stiff-upper-lip British rebelled. The British National Health Service reversed course and recently gave hospitals the ability to make their own decisions, including decisions to raise funds or float bonds to expand or buy new technologies.

Both "constrain the supply" and "low prices and fees" are centralized, micromanaging cost-control techniques. You do not have to be a die-hard capitalist to think they are bad techniques. Most left-leaning economists agree that it is better to develop incentives and let the market control costs than to have government set prices or supply.

The Problem of Politics

The third approach to cost control in a single-payer system is that adopted by Medicare in the United States: do nothing, and just pay whatever bill comes in. Let the costs go through the roof. The crisis will come later—after the current administrators and politicians are long gone. This is probably why a *New York Times* editorial said, "Even in fantasy, no one has yet come up with a way to pay for Medicare."

These three options are what most single-payer systems in the world have done. None works, and all have long-term consequences.

As Michael Millenson, a health policy consultant, remarks, when single-payer advocates think about who would run the national health plan, they think of [Democratic senator Edward M.] Ted Kennedy. But, he asks, what if the head were [Republican vice president] Dick Cheney? Medicare reveals what is likely to happen if we have a single-payer plan. Every Medicare decision is subject to political pressure from somewhere. When Medicare tries to lower hospital fees or equalize payments, hospitals pressure their representatives and senators for increases in payments. Patient advocacy groups lobby to have Medicare pay for their favorite technology or treatment. Drug companies use campaign contributions—and patient advocacy groups—to prevent a Medicare formulary and forbid price negotiations that might limit their profits. The result is that Medicare decisions are made slowly, and rarely on their merits. No federal administrative agency can be completely free of political influence. But single-payer reform plans tend to ignore the importance of administrative independence.

The ideal reform must address not only the inequitable, inefficient, and unsustainable financing system, but also the fragmented delivery system. And it must develop a plan that creates an accountable and innovative delivery system overseen by a (relatively) independent agency that can make hard administrative choices.

Consumer-Driven Universal Health Care Is the Best Solution

Regina Herzlinger

Regina Herzlinger is the Nancy R. McPherson Professor of Business Administration at Harvard Business School. She is the author of Who Killed Health Care? America's $2 Trillion Medical Problem—and the Consumer-Driven Cure.

The time for universal health insurance coverage has come. Everybody seems to know that—except for the Republicans, all too many of whom cling to traditional denunciations of universal coverage as socialism. Senate Finance Committee Chairman Max Baucus has been holding talks with Republican lawmakers over the past week [April 2009], and all signs point to opposition from the GOP [Republican Party].

The Option of Republican Universal Coverage

But for the welfare of the country and their political party, Republicans should, instead, seize the lesson of [President Richard] Nixon's trip to China. With one brilliant foray, Nixon converted the massive threat posed by the isolated China into an asset, secured a favorable mention in history, and stripped the Democrats of a key issue. By embracing their own brand of universal health coverage, Republicans can do the same. There's a massive constituency behind the policy. Buffeted by the recession and the threat of losing their employer-provided health insurance, the American people want universal coverage. Much of the US business community wants it too. CEOs [chief executive officers] rarely say "Know what I love about

Regina Herzlinger, "Why Republicans Should Back Universal Health Care," *Atlantic*, April 13, 2009. Reproduced by permission of the author.

my job? Buying health care." The chore is so unrewarding—corporate buyers have failed to create effective cost or quality improvements—that many small business CEOs simply skip it. As a result, millions distort the efficient allocation of labor in our economy by opting for jobs in dying, big companies that offer health insurance, rather than productive ones in small companies that do not. Furthermore, our employer-based health insurance system forces American businesses to pack our massive health care costs—about 70 percent greater as a share of GDP [gross domestic product] than other countries'—into the cost of their exports, a huge albatross in a globally competitive economy.

The Republicans can do a Nixon-goes-to-China by offering a better version of universal coverage. There is, after all, substantial concern about the Democrats' reliance on universal coverage through a government-controlled system like Medicare. Some distrust government's ability to make good on its promises. Medicare currently owes $36 trillion in services to those who paid for its use when they hit 65. Have you seen a spare $36 trillion hanging around? (For perspective, that amount is equivalent to about three years of US GDP.)

A Government-Controlled System

Another concern is that government will control costs by rationing health care to the sick. The government-controlled UK [United Kingdom] health care system, for example, has the lowest uptake of cancer drugs among the five biggest European economies and correspondingly low cancer survival rates. Concerns about rationing are not demagoguery. How else can a government control costs? Many experts dismiss as wishful thinking the Democrats' claims of achieving efficiency by implementing dazzling information technology and other technocratic tools. And because the truly sick constitute only 20 percent of health care users, but account for 80 percent of health care costs, they may as well wear a bull's eye on their backs: They are a politically vulnerable target for cost control through rationing.

Transforming the government into a monopolistic buyer of health care will also affect the supply of doctors. All too many doctors, saddled with massive educational debts, refuse to see Medicaid patients because they are [paid] so little. But if government were the only payer, some prospective physicians, facing the prospect of incomes totally controlled by the government, would reluctantly enter other professions.

Republicans can do a Nixon-goes-to-China by offering a better version of universal coverage.

Finally, a government-controlled system would likely impair the medically and economically important genomic sector. US venture capitalists have provided billions for research that may provide cures or even preventions for genetically linked diseases. Kiss that money—and the important personalized medicine industry it could create—goodbye under a system of government-controlled universal coverage. Venture capitalists will find it too risky to invest in markets where one payer controls prices.

A Consumer-Controlled System

The Republicans could instead offer a consumer-controlled universal coverage system, like that in Switzerland, in which the people, not the government, control how much they spend on health. There are no government health insurance programs. Instead, the Swiss choose from about 85 private health insurers. Rather than being stuffed into the degrading Medicaid program, the Swiss poor shop for health insurance like everyone else, using funds transferred to them by the government. The sick are not discriminated against either—they pay the same prices as everyone else in their demographic category. Like the US, Switzerland is a confederation of states that, as in the US, oversee the insurance system. Enforcement by the tax authorities has produced 99 percent enrollment.

This consumer-driven, universal coverage system provides excellent health care for the sick, tops the world in consumer satisfaction, and costs 40 percent less, as a percentage of GDP, than the system in the US. The Swiss could spend even less by choosing cheaper, high-deductible health insurance policies, but they have opted against doing so. Swiss consumers reward insurers that offer the best value for the money. These competitive pressures cause Swiss insurers to spend only about 5 percent on general and administrative expenses, as compared to 12–15 percent in the US. And unlike Medicare, the private Swiss firms must function without incurring massive unfunded liabilities. Competition has also pushed Swiss providers to be more efficient than those in the US. Yet they remain well-compensated.

We can also learn from the mistakes made by the Swiss. For example, they pay providers for fragmented care, rather than for integrated treatments for diseases or disabilities. The Swiss sustain an inefficient hospital sector, and they aren't transparent about the cost and quality of providers.

The Republicans could instead offer a consumer-controlled universal coverage system, like that in Switzerland.

Republicans could enact Swiss-style universal coverage by enabling employees to cash out of their employer-sponsored health insurance. (Although many view employer-sponsored health insurance as a "free" benefit, it is money that would otherwise be paid as income.) The substantial sums involved would command attention and gratitude: a 2006 cash out would have yielded $12,000—the average cost of employer-sponsored health insurance—thus raising the income of joint filers who earn less than $73,000 (90 percent of all filers) by at least 16 percent. Employees could remain in with an employer's plan or use this new income to buy their own health insurance.

The Republican choice is clear. They can whine while the Democratic Congress enacts a government-controlled system, or they can embrace a Republican approach to universal coverage.

A Consumer-Driven Health Care System Is Not the Solution

Elise Gould

Elise Gould is director of the race, ethnicity and the economy program at the Economic Policy Institute, a nonprofit think tank.

Health costs are reducing the ability of American business to compete internationally. At the same time, companies that do provide health insurance to their workers are finding it harder to compete with domestic companies that do not. Premium costs have increased on average 11.4 percent over each of the last five years [2001–2005], while overall inflation grew by just 2.5 percent and real GDP [gross domestic product] grew by 2.6 percent.

Add to that the cost of retiree coverage, and it's clear that high health care costs have become an albatross for many American companies.

Consumer-Driven Health Care

Top policy makers have suggested the answer to this problem is "consumer-driven health care," with its requisite high deductibles and health savings accounts. There are two main reasons why this isn't the answer.

First, workers don't want these plans. According to a Kaiser Family Foundation's survey of employers, only 15 percent of employees who were offered health savings accounts qualified high-deductible health plans decided to enroll. Furthermore, a study by the Commonwealth Fund shows lower satis-

Elise Gould, "Consumer-Driven Health Care Is a False Promise," *Executive Counsel Magazine*, September/October, 2006. Reproduced by permission of the Economic Policy Institute.

faction in these types of plans. It finds that 63 percent of individuals with comprehensive health insurance were extremely or very satisfied with their health plan, compared with 42 percent of consumer-driven health plan enrollees and 33 percent of high-deductible health plan participants. Granted, the status quo isn't the best option, but low take-up and low user-satisfaction should give employers pause before they decide to rearrange their benefits to offer these types of plans.

At the same time, compelling evidence suggests these consumer-driven health plans will be ineffective in restraining health costs. The ideology behind consumer-driven health care is the belief that Americans overconsume health care. Labeling this a "moral hazard" problem, proponents push for high-deductible health plans that make consumers spend out of pocket for the first dollar of coverage up to the plan deductible.

However, the large increases in health care expenditures are on big-ticket spending. It's not one more visit a year to the doctor that's driving these costs, or one extra test, or the choice of one doctor over another. The top 20 percent of health spenders account for 80 percent of all health spending. These are people with chronic conditions or costly hospitalizations. By definition, the vast majority of high spending is above the region where these incentives lie.

High-Deductible Health Plans

High-deductible health plans seem to reduce health expenditures because individuals pay the full cost of their health consumption up to the deductible. But contributions to health saving accounts are tax-deductible, and the tax deductibility essentially works as a government subsidy, thus reducing their actual cost-effectiveness. Furthermore, people with high-deductible plans may delay care and end up with serious conditions that might have been prevented.

Current proposals that would raise the deductible contribution limit to health savings accounts really do nothing to reduce health costs, and may increase them. These plans can be viewed, basically, as retirement savings tax shelters for healthy people. If the point is to provide another tax shelter, fine, but this is not a way to lower health costs for businesses or individuals.

Compelling evidence suggests these consumer-driven health plans will be ineffective in restraining health costs.

Companies with several plan options should be wary of introducing high-deductible health plans for another reason: They shift costs from one group of employees to another, but are unlikely to reduce costs for the business. The healthier employees are more likely to prefer the high-deductible health plans, because they expect to consume less health care, while the less healthy will prefer more conventional plans with comprehensive coverage. If healthier employees leave conventional health plans, it will drive up the cost of insuring the less healthy workers. As a result, there may be no cost savings with a high-deductible health plan.

The Individual Market

Employers do gain from a healthier workforce. A healthier, insured workforce is likely to be more productive, with fewer absences and sick days, and with less turnover.

The solution to the U.S. health care problem should involve increasing the size of pools, not decreasing them. Contrary to a frequently made claim, encouraging people to purchase in the individual market will not by itself achieve the goal of a healthy and insured workforce. Someone with chronic health problems or preexisting conditions—or who has family members in those categories—will find it nearly impossible to get adequate coverage in the individual market.

Individual insurance companies set rates based on health status and medical history. If you are healthy one year but get sick the next, you will find it more difficult to get good coverage and your rates will go up.

In contrast, pooling and community rating spreads the risks over large groups. In a given year, a large percentage of the pool won't get sick, and the insurance company will be able to maintain profitability, smoothing risk over many individuals or large groups. The result: People keep their coverage, with predictable costs and with continuity of care.

If consumer-driven health care, high-deductible health plans, and the individual market are not the magic bullet that proponents claim, then where are businesses to turn as health costs continue to rise to the point where their survival is threatened?

Universal Coverage

Perhaps it's time to consider universal coverage. Universal coverage, in a variety of forms, can create the workforce businesses want for little more than they pay for health insurance now. Universal coverage aids businesses by lowering administrative costs for employers and health care providers. Instead of each company having to administer its own health plans, and health providers having to hire insurance personnel to navigate the nightmarishly complex system we have today, a more centralized system can capitalize on consolidated filing and reimbursement mechanisms, thus saving money.

Encouraging people to purchase in the individual market will not by itself achieve the goal of a healthy and insured workforce.

Coverage provided outside the work environment can also allow businesses to enjoy greater flexibility in the workforce. They can hire workers at whatever hours they find most efficient, choose from a pool of better-qualified part-time employees, and avoid having to deal with the high fixed costs of hiring full-time employees. Universal coverage can create risk pools that small businesses can't achieve, and at prices they can afford.

Moreover, a system run at the federal or state level can allow government to negotiate prices and provide incentives for the use of evidence-based medicine, enforce best practices, and encourage cost savings through disease prevention and chronic disease management. Perhaps it's time for U.S. business to take the lead and move this country into the 21st century, joining other developed countries in providing basic coverage to all.

Organizations to Contact

The editors have compiled the following list of organizations concerned with the issues debated in this book. The descriptions are derived from materials provided by the organizations. All have publications or information available for interested readers. The list was compiled on the date of publication of the present volume; the information provided here may change. Be aware that many organizations take several weeks or longer to respond to inquiries, so allow as much time as possible.

Alliance for Health Reform
1444 Eye Street NW, Suite 910, Washington, DC   20005-6573
(202) 789-2300 • fax: (202) 789-2233
e-mail: info@allhealth.org
Web site: www.allhealth.org

The Alliance for Health Reform exists to provide unbiased information to understand the roots of the nation's health care problems and the trade-offs posed by competing proposals for change. The Alliance for Health Reform believes that everyone in the United States should have health coverage at a reasonable cost, but rather than taking positions on legislation, the organization focuses its efforts on holding informational forums. The Alliance for Health Reform produces issue briefs regularly on topics such as "Covering the Uninsured: Options for Reform."

Alliance to Defend Health Care
1534 Tremont Street, Boston, MA   02120
(617) 784-6367
e-mail: contact@defendhealth.org

The Alliance to Defend Health Care is a group of health care professionals and others who believe that health care is a fundamental human right and that the delivery of health care should be guided by science and compassion, not by corporate self-interest. The alliance collaborates with others to foster a broad public dialogue and health policy reforms to achieve universal access to high-quality, affordable health care for all.

American Enterprise Institute for Public Policy Research (AEI)

1150 Seventeenth Street NW, Washington, DC   20036
(202) 862-5800 • fax: (202) 862-7177
e-mail: info@aei.org
Web site: www.aei.org

The American Enterprise Institute for Public Policy Research (AEI) is a private, nonpartisan, nonprofit institution dedicated to research and education on issues of government, politics, economics, and social welfare. AEI sponsors research and publishes materials toward defending the principles and improving the institutions of American freedom and democratic capitalism. Among AEI's publications are the Health Policy Outlook Series and the books *Innovation and Technology Adoption in Health Care Markets* and *Bring Market Prices to Medicare.*

Campaign for an American Solution

601 Pennsylvania Avenue NW, South Building, Suite 500
Washington, DC   20004
(202) 778-3200 • fax: (202) 331-7487
e-mail: info@americanhealthsolution.org
Web site: www.americanhealthsolution.org

Campaign for an American Solution is a campaign sponsored by America's Health Insurance Plans (AHIP), the national trade association for health insurance companies. The mission of the Campaign for an American Solution is to build support for workable health care reform based on core principles supported by the American people, and it works to facilitate a constructive conversation to that end. The campaign has published a health care proposal, *Now Is the Time for Health Care Reform: A Proposal to Achieve Universal Coverage, Affordability, Quality Improvement, and Market Reform*, which is available at its Web site.

Cato Institute
1000 Massachusetts Avenue NW
Washington, DC   20001-5403
(202) 842-0200 • fax: (202) 842-3490
Web site: www.cato.org

The Cato Institute is a public policy research foundation dedicated to limiting the role of government, protecting individual liberties, and promoting free markets. Cato has been a longtime advocate of deregulating the health care industry, so that consumers can afford the health care insurance and treatment of their choice. Among the center's publications is the book *Healthy Competition: What's Holding Back Health Care and How to Free It.*

Commonwealth Fund
1 East Seventy-fifth Street, New York, NY   10021
(212) 606-3800 • fax: (212) 606-3500
e-mail: info@cmwf.org
Web site: www.commonwealthfund.org

The Commonwealth Fund is a private foundation that aims to promote a high-performing health care system that achieves better access, improved quality, and greater efficiency, particularly for society's most vulnerable, including low-income people, the uninsured, minority Americans, young children, and elderly adults. The Commonwealth Fund carries out this mandate by supporting independent research on health care issues and developing grants to improve health care practice and policy. The foundation produces more than one hundred publications per year, including an annual report and *The Commonwealth Fund Connection*, which are available on its Web site.

Georgetown Health Policy Institute
Georgetown University, Washington, DC 20057-1485
(202) 687-0880 • fax: (202) 687-3110
Web site: http://ihcrp.georgetown.edu

The Georgetown Health Policy Institute is a multidisciplinary group of faculty and staff dedicated to conducting research on key issues in health policy and health services research. Projects focus on health care financing, the uninsured, federal health insurance reforms, quality of care and outcomes research, mental health services research, and the impact of changes in the health care market on providers and patients. Publications sponsored by the institute include "Medicaid and State Budgets: Looking at the Facts."

Health Care for America Now (HCAN)
1825 K Street NW, Suite 400, Washington, DC 20006
(202) 454-6200
e-mail: info@healthcareforamericanow.org
Web site: www.healthcareforamericanow.org

Health Care for America Now (HCAN) is a national grassroots campaign of more than one thousand organizations in forty-six states representing 30 million people dedicated to winning quality, affordable health care. HCAN works to mobilize people in their communities to lobby their U.S. senators and representatives in Congress to stand up to the insurance companies and other special interest groups to achieve quality, affordable health care. HCAN publishes numerous reports, including "Health Insurers Falsely Claim Rising Costs Justify Soaring Premiums."

Healthcare-NOW!
1315 Spruce Street, Philadelphia, PA 19107
(800) 453-1305
e-mail: info@healthcare-now.org
Web site: www.healthcare-now.org

Healthcare-NOW! is an education and advocacy organization that addresses the health insurance crisis in the United States. Healthcare-NOW! advocates for the passage of national, single-payer health care legislation, specifically campaigning for the National Health Care Act, H.R. 676. Available at the organization's Web site is the full text of the proposed legislation.

Heartland Institute

19 South LaSalle Street #903, Chicago, IL   60603
(312) 377-4000 • fax: (312) 377-5000
e-mail: publications@heartland.org
Web site: www.heartland.org

The mission of the Heartland Institute is to discover and promote free market solutions to social and economic problems. The Heartland Institute's Health Care Policy Issue Suite is a comprehensive resource for people who support a free market approach to improving the nation's health care system. The institute publishes *Consumer Power Report* and *Health Care News*, its national outreach publications for the consumer-driven health care movement; *Heartland Policy Studies*, peer-reviewed original research on health care topics; and *Research & Commentary*, collections of the best available research on hot topics in the health care reform debate.

Physicians for a National Health Program (PNHP)

29 E. Madison, Suite 602, Chicago, IL   60602
(312) 782-6006 • fax: (312) 782-6007
e-mail: info@pnhp.org
Web site: www.pnhp.org

Physicians for a National Health Program (PNHP) is a nonprofit research and education organization of seventeen thousand physicians, medical students, and health professionals who support single-payer national health insurance. PNHP performs research on the need for fundamental health care system reform, coordinates speakers and forums, participates in town hall meetings and debates, contributes scholarly articles to peer-reviewed medical journals, and appears regularly on national television and news programs advocating for a single-payer system. Among the research papers sponsored by PNHP is "Illness and Injury as Contributors to Bankruptcy."

Urban Institute
2100 M Street NW, Washington, DC   20037
(202) 833-7200
Web site: www.urban.org

The Urban Institute works to foster sound public policy and effective government by gathering data, conducting research, evaluating programs, offering technical assistance overseas, and educating Americans on social and economic issues. The Urban Institute's Health Policy Center analyzes trends and underlying causes of changes in health insurance coverage, access to care, and use of health care services by the entire U.S. population. The Urban Institute publishes a variety of resources, including books such as *Health Policy and the Uninsured*.

Bibliography

Books

Donald L. Barlett and James B. Steele *Critical Condition: How Health Care in America Became Big Business—and Bad Medicine.* New York: Broadway, 2005.

Roger M. Battistella *Health Care Turning Point: Why Single Payer Won't Work.* Cambridge, MA: MIT Press, 2010.

Shannon Brownlee *Overtreated: Why Too Much Medicine Is Making Us Sicker and Poorer.* New York: Bloomsbury, 2007.

Michael F. Cannon and Michael D. Tanner *Healthy Competition: What's Holding Back Health Care and How to Free It.* 2nd ed. Washington, DC: Cato Institute, 2007.

John F. Cogan, R. Glenn Hubbard, and Daniel P. Kessler *Healthy, Wealthy, and Wise: Five Steps to a Better Health Care System.* Washington, DC: AEI Press, 2005.

Jonathan Cohn *Sick: The Untold Story of America's Health Care Crisis—and the People Who Pay the Price.* New York: Harper Perennial, 2008.

Tom Daschle, with Scott S. Greenberger and Jeanne M. Lambrew — *Critical: What We Can Do About the Health-Care Crisis.* New York: Thomas Dunne, 2008.

Ezekiel J. Emanuel — *Healthcare, Guaranteed: A Simple, Secure Solution for America.* New York: PublicAffairs, 2008.

Arthur Garson Jr. and Carolyn L. Engelhard — *Health Care Half-Truths: Too Many Myths, Not Enough Reality.* Lanham, MD: Rowman & Littlefield, 2007.

David Gratzer — *Why Obama's Government Takeover of Health Care Will Be a Disaster.* New York: Encounter Books, 2009.

George C. Halvorson — *Health Care Will Not Reform Itself: A User's Guide to Refocusing and Reforming American Health Care.* New York: CRC Press, 2009.

Regina E. Herzlinger — *Who Killed Health Care? America's $2 Trillion Medical Problem—and the Consumer-Driven Cure.* New York: McGraw-Hill, 2007.

Steven Jonas, Raymond Goldsteen, and Karen Goldsteen — *An Introduction to the U.S. Health Care System.* 6th ed. New York: Springer, 2007.

Arnold Kling — *Crisis of Abundance: Rethinking How We Pay for Health Care.* Washington, DC: Cato Institute, 2006.

Phillip Longman — *Best Care Anywhere: Why VA Health Care Is Better than Yours.* Sausalito, CA: PoliPointPress, 2007.

Michael E. Porter and Elizabeth Olmsted Teisberg — *Redefining Health Care: Creating Value-Based Competition on Results.* Cambridge, MA: Harvard Business School Press, 2006.

Arnold Relman — *A Second Opinion: Rescuing America's Health Care.* New York: PublicAffairs, 2007.

J. Patrick Rooney and Dan Perrin — *America's Health Care Crisis Solved: Money-Saving Solutions, Coverage for Everyone.* Hoboken, NJ: Wiley, 2008.

Periodicals

Joseph Antos and Alice M. Rivlin — "Slowing the Rising Costs of Health Care Possible," *Times-Union* (Albany, NY), April 1, 2007.

Scott Atlas — "10 Surprising Facts About American Health Care," National Center for Policy Analysis, Brief Analysis no. 649, March 24, 2009. www.ncpa.org.

Ronald Bailey — "Your Money or Your Life: Medical Spending Still a Good Value," *Reason Online*, September 15, 2006. www.reason.com.

Billy Beane, Newt Gingrich, and John Kerry — "How to Take American Health Care from Worst to First," *New York Times*, October 24, 2008.

Sandra G. Boodman	"Seeing Red: The Rising Costs of Care and a Failing Economy Drive More Americans into Medical Debt," *Washington Post*, January 13, 2009.
Donald J. Boudreaux	"The Way to Better, Cheaper Healthcare: Don't Make It a Human Right," *Christian Science Monitor*, October 17, 2006.
David Broder	"For a Change, Movement on Health Care Reform," *Record* (Bergen County, NJ), November 29, 2008.
Deborah Burger	"On Health Care Reform: Long Waits Are Really Sicko," *San Francisco Chronicle*, July 10, 2007.
John E. Calfee	"Six Ways Not to Reform Health Care," *Health Policy Outlook*, no. 1, January 2010.
Kevin Cape	"French Health Care Problematic in U.S.," *Register-Guard* (Eugene, OR), August 19, 2007.
Christianity Today	"The Health Care Crunch: Let's Make Sure Any Reform Plan We Pursue Avoids the Single-Value Syndrome," February 5, 2008.
Mark B. Constantian	"Where U.S. Health Care Ranks Number One," *Wall Street Journal*, January 7, 2010.
Clive Crook	"The Long Road to Healthcare Reform," *Financial Times*, December 15, 2008.

Theodore Dalrymple	"Health of the State: Doctors, Patients, and Michael Moore," *National Review*, August 13, 2007.
Karen Davis	"The Way Forward with Health Reform," Commonwealth Fund, January 28, 2010. www.commonwealthfund.org.
Rose Ann DeMoro	"Obama and Daschle Should Opt for Single-Payer," *Progressive*, December 11, 2008.
Milt Freudenheim	"With Health Care Topic A, Some Sketches for a Solution," *New York Times*, January 25, 2007.
Arthur Garson Jr.	"Healthcare's Wasted Billions," *Christian Science Monitor*, October 8, 2008.
Atul Gawande	"Sick and Twisted," *New Yorker*, July 23, 2007.
Newt Gingrich and Sheldon Whitehouse	"Next President Must Put Health in Health Care," *Washington Times*, October 28, 2008.
Lisa Girion	"Healthy? Insurers Don't Buy It: Minor Ailments Can Thwart Applicants for Individual Policies," *Los Angeles Times*, December 31, 2006.
Peter Glusker	"Universal Health Care That's Not-for-Profit Can Work," *National Catholic Reporter*, September 21, 2007.

Amy Goodman   "Nothing to Fear but No Health Care," *Seattle Times*, January 15, 2009.

Scott Gottlieb   "What Medicaid Tells Us About Government Health Care," *Wall Street Journal*, January 8, 2009.

Daniel Gross   "National Health Care? We're Halfway There," *New York Times*, December 3, 2006.

Jacob S. Hacker   "Better Medicine," *Slate*, October 10, 2006. www.slate.com.

Regina Herzlinger   "America, Insure Thyself," *Washington Post*, March 29, 2008.

Jacob G. Hornberger   "Health Care Is Not a Right," Future of Freedom Foundation, July 1, 2009. www.fff.org.

Paul Hsieh   "Universal Healthcare and the Waistline Police," *Christian Science Monitor*, January 7, 2009.

Sue Hutchison   "Health Care Reform Needed to Keep Saving Lives Like These," *San Jose Mercury News*, February 5, 2008.

David Iverson and Elinor Christiansen   "Single-Payer Health Care Is Way to Go," *Rocky Mountain News* (Denver, CO), September 4, 2006.

Stephen Kemble   "For Healthcare, Single-Payer System Is Best," *Honolulu Advertiser*, January 23, 2009.

Michael Kinsley   "To Your Health: Why Modest
                   Reform Is Preferable to Single-Payer
                   Health Care," *Slate*, March 17, 2006.

Paul Krugman   "The Health Care Crisis and What to
and Robin Wells   Do About It," *New York Review of
                   Books*, February 22, 2006.

Darrell Laurant   "Is Health Care Really That Bad?"
                   News & Advance (Lynchburg, VA),
                   November 24, 2008.

Mary Jo Layton   "Ripping Off Dr. America," *Record*
                   (Bergen County, NJ), June 10, 2007.

David Lazarus   "Major Surgery Is the Only Cure,"
                   San Francisco Chronicle, October 1,
                   2006.

Betsy McCaughey   "The Truth About Mandatory Health
                   Insurance," *Wall Street Journal*,
                   January 4, 2008.

Charles R. Morris "Health Care for All: Not Easy, Not
                   Cheap, but Possible," *Commonweal*,
                   August 15, 2008.

Patt Morrison   "Insurance Is Enough to Make You
                   Sick; Private Health Insurance Is a
                   Drag on the Economy the
                   Government Must Fix," *Los Angeles
                   Times*, January 4, 2007.

New Republic   "Moral Imperative," March 19, 2006.

New York Times   "The High Cost of Health Care,"
                   November 25, 2007.

Timothy Noah   "Time to Socialize Medicine," *Slate*,
                    November 8, 2006. www.slate.com.

Michael E. Porter   "Information Is the Best Medicine:
and Elizabeth   Doctor Know," *New Republic*, July
Olmsted Teisberg   2006.

Tom Price   "Transforming Health Care: Provide
                    Access and Ownership to Patients
                    First," *Washington Times*, July 31,
                    2008.

Waldo Proffitt   "HMOs a Model? Hardly," *Sarasota
                    Herald Tribune*, October 8, 2006.

Jane Bryant   "We Can Afford Universal Health
Quinn   Care," *Newsweek*, July 30, 2007.

Register-Guard   "The Best Health Care Plan," March
(Eugene, OR)   2, 2008.

Kate Riley   "Nibbling at the Edges of Health
                    Care," *Seattle Times*, January 21,
                    2008.

Mike Seate   "Time Has Arrived for Universal
                    Health Care," *Pittsburgh
                    Tribune-Review*, March 4, 2008.

Donna Smith   "2.6 Million New American Jobs and
                    a Working Healthcare System . . .
                    Who Knew?" CommonDreams.org,
                    January 15, 2009.

Richard Smith   "Everyone Could Be a Winner,"
                    Guardian (UK), November 6, 2006.

Michael D.
Tanner

"The Great Wait," *National Review,*
September 13, 2006.

Ken Terry

"On Health Care Reform: For
Employers, There's No Exit from
Health Care," *San Francisco Chronicle,*
July 10, 2007.

Daniel Weintraub

"Sales Tax for Health Care Plan Poses
a Dilemma," *Sacramento Bee,*
September 16, 2007.

Matt Welch

"Why I Prefer French Health Care,"
Reason, January 2010.

Index

I

M

Malpractice effects, health care costs, 48, 53, 55
Mammograms, 41–42
Managed care programs, 138
  See also HMOs (health maintenance organizations)
Mandates for health insurance
  constitutional, 68–72
  employers, con- stance, 86–93
  employers, pro- stance, 73–76
  hardship exemptions, 118
  reform bill differences, 94
  state attempts, 84–85, 148
  violation of liberty/ unconstitutional, 81–85, 91–93
Mandatory benefits, 133
Massachusetts
  employer coverage policy, 76
  mandate for coverage, 84–85
  premium costs, 59
  subsidized care, 22, 76, 130, 148
Mayo Clinic, 56
McCanne, Don, 140–145
McCarran-Ferguson Act (1945), 63
Medicaid, 20, 127–128, 137
  government control, 129–130
  prices and rates, 131, 153, 158
  spending increases, 138, 147
  tax support and eligibility, 131
Medical errors
  deaths, 25
  patient perceptions, 32–33
Medical record centralization, 33, 164
Medical research funding, 158
Medicare, 20, 40, 137

chronic diseases costs, 25
government control, 59, 129–130, 150
illegal immigration issues, 77
Inspector General cost estimates, 150–151
Part A, 128
Part B, 111, 155
passage, 1965, 14, 126, 128
politics, 154–155
prices and rates, 59, 114, 119, 127, 128–129, 131, 150, 153, 154–155
public option comparisons, 99, 103, 109, 111–112, 126, 127, 128–130, 131, 139, 157
single-payer option comparisons, 143, 150, 151
spending increases, 138
unnecessary care, 49, 50–51
Medicare Advantage plans, 111, 113
Medicare Payment Advisory Commission (MedPAC), 111–112, 114
Medigap coverage, 111
Menopause, 52
Miller, Tom, 128
Minimum wage, 72
Moffit, Robert, 81–85
Monopolies. *See* Consolidation and monopolies, health care industry
Montana, 116
Moore, Michael, 29, 31
Mortality. *See* Infant mortality; Life expectancy and rankings; Preventable deaths, U.S.
Murphy family (Sandy and Charlie), 46

N

National health care programs. *See*
Canada; Single-payer plans;
United Kingdom
New Deal programs, 126
Nixon, Richard M., 14, 156
Noah, Timothy, 68–72
Nonelective surgery waiting time,
32
North Dakota, 116

O

Obama, Barack (and
administration)
employer-provided health
care, opinions, 86
health care and immigration
policy, 77–78, 80
health care reform finance,
25–26, 57–60, 81, 129
health care reform/public option support, 26–28, 63, 81,
115, 126–127, 131–133
health care reform studies,
57–58
mandated health insurance,
68–69, 81–85, 86–87, 88,
90–93
Patient Protection and Affordable Care Act, 14–17
Obesity, 19–20, 136
Oregon, state programs, 130
Organisation for Economic Co-
operation and Development
(OECD)
chronic condition care, 42
life expectancy average, 40
preventive care, 42, 45
Organization-provided health insurance, 92

Out-of-pocket costs
health system ranking factor,
34
increases, 135
insurance companies variation, 106
overtreatment examples, 46,
47
See also Co-pays; Premiums
Overtreatment
consumer choices, 48–49
consumer-driven plans as cor-
rective, 162
harms to patients, 49, 51–52
reasons, 52–54
U.S. health care system, and
costs, 46–56, 59, 147–148
Overview, U.S. health care, 19–22,
135–139

P

Paperless health information tech-
nology, 25, 55
Patient complaints, 34
Patient demands, perceptions,
52–53
Patient Protection and Affordable
Care Act (2010), 14–17
Per-person spending, United
States, 19, 24, 141
Peron, James, 29–34
Pharmaceutical industry
advertising, 52
obstructions, health care
reform/public option, 115,
155
single-payer system price ne-
gotiation, 148–149
Physician choice, 27, 33
Physician groups, 147